Health and Fitness

Opposing Viewpoints®

Other Books of Related Interest

Opposing Viewpoints Series

An Aging Population
AIDS
America Beyond 2001
America's Children
America's Victims
Biomedical Ethics
Chemical Dependency
Death and Dying
Drug Abuse
The Environment
Euthanasia
Health Care in America
Human Sexuality
Mental Illness
Population
Poverty
21st Century Earth
Violence

Current Controversies Series

The AIDS Crisis
Alcoholism
Family Violence
Hunger
Reproductive Technologies

At Issues Series

Domestic Violence
Environmental Justice
Legalizing Drugs
Rape on Campus
Smoking

*H*ealth
*F*and itness

Opposing Viewpoints®

David Bender & Bruno Leone, *Series Editors*

Scott Barbour, *Book Editor*
Karin L. Swisher, *Book Editor*

OPPOSING
VIEWPOINTS®
SERIES

Greenhaven Press, Inc., San Diego, CA

Cover photo: Gazelle Technologies

Greenhaven Press, Inc.
PO Box 289009
San Diego, CA 92198-9009

Library of Congress Cataloging-in-Publication Data

Health and fitness : opposing viewpoints / Scott Barbour, book
    editor, Karin L. Swisher, book editor.
        p.   cm. — (Opposing viewpoints series)
    Includes bibliographical references (p.   ) and index.
    ISBN 1-56510-403-X (lib. bdg. : alk. paper). —
ISBN 1-56510-402-1 (pbk. : alk. paper)
    I.
    Barbour, Scott, 1963–   . II. Swisher, Karin, 1966–
III. Series: Opposing viewpoints series (Unnumbered)

Every effort has been made to trace the owners of copyrighted material.

"Congress shall make no law . . .
abridging the freedom of speech,
or of the press."

First Amendment to the U.S. Constitution

The basic foundation of our democracy is the First Amendment
guarantee of freedom of expression. The Opposing Viewpoints
Series is dedicated to the concept of this basic freedom and the
idea that it is more important to practice it than to enshrine it.

Contents

Why Consider Opposing Viewpoints?

"The only way in which a human being can make some approach to knowing the whole of a subject is by hearing what can be said about it by persons of every variety of opinion and studying all modes in which it can be looked at by every character of mind. No wise man ever acquired his wisdom in any mode but this."

John Stuart Mill

In our media-intensive culture it is not difficult to find differing opinions. Thousands of newspapers and magazines and dozens of radio and television talk shows resound with differing points of view. The difficulty lies in deciding which opinion to agree with and which "experts" seem the most credible. The more inundated we become with differing opinions and claims, the more essential it is to hone critical reading and thinking skills to evaluate these ideas. Opposing Viewpoints books address this problem directly by presenting stimulating debates that can be used to enhance and teach these skills. The varied opinions contained in each book examine many different aspects of a single issue. While examining these conveniently edited opposing views, readers can develop critical thinking skills such as the ability to compare and contrast authors' credibility, facts, argumentation styles, use of persuasive techniques, and other stylistic tools. In short, the Opposing Viewpoints Series is an ideal way to attain the higher-level thinking and reading skills so essential in a culture of diverse and contradictory opinions.

In addition to providing a tool for critical thinking, Opposing Viewpoints books challenge readers to question their own strongly held opinions and assumptions. Most people form their opinions on the basis of upbringing, peer pressure, and personal, cultural, or professional bias. By reading carefully balanced opposing views, readers must directly confront new ideas as well as the opinions of those with whom they disagree. This is not to simplistically argue that everyone who reads opposing views will—or should—change his or her opinion. Instead, the series enhances readers' depth of understanding of their own views by encouraging confrontation with opposing ideas. Careful examination of others' views can lead to the readers' understanding of the logical inconsistencies in their own opinions, perspective on why they hold an opinion, and the consideration of the possibility that their opinion requires further evaluation.

Evaluating Other Opinions

To ensure that this type of examination occurs, Opposing Viewpoints books present all types of opinions. Prominent spokespeople on different sides of each issue as well as well-known professionals from many disciplines challenge the reader. An additional goal of the series is to provide a forum for other, less known, or even unpopular viewpoints. The opinion of an ordinary person who has had to make the decision to cut off life support from a terminally ill relative, for example, may be just as valuable and provide just as much insight as a medical ethicist's professional opinion. The editors have two additional purposes in including these less known views. One, the editors encourage readers to respect others' opinions—even when not enhanced by professional credibility. It is only by reading or listening to and objectively evaluating others' ideas that one can determine whether they are worthy of consideration. Two, the inclusion of such viewpoints encourages the important critical thinking skill of objectively evaluating an author's credentials and bias. This evaluation will illuminate an author's reasons for taking a particular stance on an issue and will aid in readers' evaluation of the author's ideas.

As series editors of the Opposing Viewpoints Series, it is our hope that these books will give readers a deeper understanding of the issues debated and an appreciation of the complexity of even seemingly simple issues when good and honest people disagree. This awareness is particularly important in a democratic society such as ours in which people enter into public debate to determine the common good. Those with whom one disagrees should not be regarded as enemies but rather as people whose views deserve careful examination and may shed light on one's own.

Thomas Jefferson once said that "difference of opinion leads to inquiry, and inquiry to truth." Jefferson, a broadly educated man, argued that "if a nation expects to be ignorant and free . . . it expects what never was and never will be." As individuals and as a nation, it is imperative that we consider the opinions of others and examine them with skill and discernment. The Opposing Viewpoints Series is intended to help readers achieve this goal.

David L. Bender & Bruno Leone,
Series Editors

Introduction

"America's greatest nutritional need sometimes seems to be for accurate information."

Diane Woznicki and Hien Nguyen, Priorities, *vol. 7, no. 3, 1995*

In 1993, the Center for Science in the Public Interest (CSPI) attracted extensive media attention when it reported that Chinese restaurant food is unhealthy. A meal of kung pao chicken, the center claimed, is comparable to "four McDonald's quarter-pounders." In the months that followed this news, the CSPI focused on several other types of food—including Italian food, Mexican food, and movie-theater popcorn—that, according to the center's findings, contained unhealthy levels of salt and fat. The center declared that fettuccine Alfredo is "a heart attack on a plate," that eating "chile rellenos is like eating a whole stick of butter," and that a medium-sized container of movie-theater popcorn with butter-flavored topping contains "more fat than a bacon-and-eggs breakfast, a Big-Mac-with-fries lunch, and a steak dinner with all the trimmings combined."

In response to this ever-growing list of dangerous foods, Mike Royko, a columnist for the *Chicago Tribune*, undoubtedly expressed the frustrations of many Americans when he wrote, "I can save the Center for Science in the Public Interest a lot of bother and expense. All it takes is a simple announcement: If something tastes good, it is probably bad. If something tastes really dull, it is probably good." In a humorous tone, Royko asked, "Who knows where the food nags will strike next? A deli?" Ironically, delis were one of the CSPI's subsequent targets: It proclaimed that an egg-salad sandwich "makes a Dairy Queen banana split look like a diet food."

The CSPI's campaign against unhealthy food and the reaction to it illustrate the uneasy relationship that often exists between health experts and the American public. Health officials—with the help of the news media and advertisers—produce a constant stream of information about the health effects of various foods, beverages, chemicals, drugs, lifestyles, and activities. These reports ceaselessly implore the public to adhere to dietary and fitness guidelines that are continually being updated, revised, and amended. Because these recommendations are in constant flux—and often contradict one another—frustration such as that expressed by Royko is commonplace. Some people adopt the attitude that because risks are ubiquitous and health problems are unavoidable, it is futile to attempt to alter one's behavior to avoid the inevitable. Daniel Minturn, a shipping clerk interviewed by Richard Woodbury in *Time* magazine, succinctly summed up this philosophy as he prepared to eat a cheeseburger: "Everywhere you turn, it's a warning for this and a warning for that. So what's wrong with just now and then going out and enjoying what you want?"

In fact, health experts who challenge the CSPI's claims suggest that Minturn's attitude is the correct one. Elizabeth M. Whelan, the president of the American Council on Science and Health, argues,

> CSPI's diet advice is "lite" on science and "reduced" in common sense. It . . . overlooks the fact that what is important is one's overall diet, not the occasional consumption of any specific food. The key to healthy eating is a balanced, varied, moderate diet—and there is room in that overall scheme for fettucini and popcorn.

Whelan and others accuse the CSPI of oversimplifying nutritional science. These critics contend that the restaurant foods cited by the CSPI are safe in moderate amounts, and that the CSPI ignores the fact that the degree of risk posed by fat and salt intake varies among individuals. For example, Jacob Sullum writes in *National Review*, "While too much [salt] aggravates certain kinds of hypertension, there is no medical reason for people in general to avoid it." Similarly, he argues that although "a high-fat diet may increase the risk of heart disease in some people, . . . that does not mean that fettuccine Alfredo, kung pao chicken, and chile rellenos are poison."

Not only do experts debate the dangers posed by fat levels in particular foods, they also disagree about the risks and benefits of different types of fat. The food guide pyramid developed and issued by the U.S. Department of Agriculture (USDA) in 1992 recommends using all fats and oils "sparingly." However, according to Michael Mason, a staff writer for *Health* magazine, this advice is misguided because it fails to differentiate between kinds of fat. While saturated fat has been linked to heart disease, Mason notes, monounsaturated fat may actually benefit the cardiovascular system. Mason argues that by lumping all fats and oils together, the USDA calls for cutting olive oil, which is a source of monounsaturated fat. Simultaneously, according to Mason, while the pyramid advises cutting fats and oils, it allows for two to three servings per day of red meat, which is high in saturated fat. To rectify these inconsistencies, Mason endorses an alternative pyramid that was developed in 1994 by the Harvard School of Public Health, Oldways Prevention & Exchange Trust, and the World Health Organization. Based on the traditional Mediterranean diet, the new pyramid recommends eating red meat only a few times a month and calls for daily use of olive oil.

Along with contradictory information on nutrition, the public also receives mixed signals on exercise. For example, during the 1970s and 1980s, experts recommended that Americans engage in vigorous exercise for a minimum of thirty minutes a day, five days a week. In 1993, however, new guidelines were released jointly by the U.S. Centers for Disease Control and Prevention (CDC) and the American College of Sports Medicine (ACSM). The CDC and the ACSM called for moderate exercise and said that the recommended daily amount of activity could be "accumulated in short bouts" rather than during one workout, as was previously recommended. Then, in 1995, a study authored by I-Min Lee, an assistant professor of medicine at the Harvard School of Public Health, concluded that vigorous exercise—but not moderate exercise—was associated with greater longevity, suggesting that only vigorous exercise could help people live longer. Reflecting the public's confusion, an Associated Press article reporting on Lee's study began, "Run! No, walk. No, run!"

The uncertainty caused by such contradictory information can lead some people to become discouraged and to adopt a careless attitude about their personal health and fitness. However, amid the cacophony of competing recommendations, a few generalizations can safely be made. Most experts agree that some exercise is better than no exercise, and most agree that the best diet is a varied one low in saturated fat. In *Health and Fitness: Opposing Viewpoints*, authors examine diet, exercise, and other topics in the following chapters: What Behaviors Pose the Greatest Health Risks and Benefits? Are Exercise and Weight-Loss Treatments Beneficial? Are Alternative Therapies Viable? Is the Health Care Industry Effective? Throughout these chapters, issues that affect the health and fitness of all Americans are discussed and debated.

What Behaviors Pose the Greatest Health Risks and Benefits?

*H*ealth
and
*F*itness

Chapter Preface

In earlier generations, beef was considered essential to a healthy diet. Meat was one of the four main recommended food groups, and beef was a mainstay of that group. More recently, scientists and researchers have revealed that saturated fat plays a role in heart disease—a leading cause of death—and other major health problems, perhaps even cancer. The high fat counts in many cuts of beef (a serving of short ribs has 20 grams of saturated fat) soon gave it a bad reputation. In fact, Jeremy Rifkin of Beyond Beef, an organization dedicated to eliminating beef consumption, argues that "beef production and consumption are now major causes of . . . human disease and death."

In 1990, the United States Department of Agriculture changed its dietary recommendations from the four food groups to the food pyramid, recommending fewer servings of meat. The consumption of beef declined correspondingly, as the health-conscious reduced or eliminated beef from their diets in order to lose weight and decrease the health risks associated with eating beef. According to the American Council on Science and Health, beef consumption decreased from 89 pounds per person in 1976 to 63 pounds in 1991.

Many beef producers and consumers, however, reject the characterization of beef as being categorically bad for human health. Instead, they contend that beef can be part of a healthy diet and, in fact, provides many necessary vitamins and minerals. Kathleen Meister of the American Council on Science and Health concurs. She writes, "The idea that beef should not be included in a healthful diet is wrong." And according to biologist Paul Saltman of the University of California at San Diego, because beef has been eliminated from many diets, "millions of young American women are testing anemic. If they think they're getting enough iron from leafy green vegetables, they'd better be eating eight pounds of them a day."

The health risks and/or benefits of eating beef are among the issues debated in the following chapter.

"Beef is a significant source of many nutrients that are essential to good health."

Eating Meat Is Healthy

Beef Industry Council

The Beef Industry Council, a division of the National Live Stock and Meat Board, is a meat-industry organization that promotes beef consumption. In the following viewpoint, the council maintains that beef is a source of many nutrients necessary for human health, including iron, zinc, and several vitamins. The council also contends that the quality of beef has improved in recent years and that the fat and cholesterol levels of beef are comparable to those of chicken.

As you read, consider the following questions:

1. What is the "meat factor," according to the council?
2. According to the council, what percentage of the daily recommended allowance of iron is provided by a three-ounce portion of beef?
3. How many milligrams of cholesterol are contained in a three-ounce portion of lean beef, according to the council?

There is good news about beef. Through the combined efforts of ranchers and farmers, packers and retailers, leaner cattle are being brought to market, and more closely trimmed beef cuts are sold at the retail counter.

The industry is also helping shoppers select and cook leaner beef cuts, by providing more nutrition information at the meat counter and by promoting quick, streamlined cooking methods. . . .

Balance, Variety, Moderation

Beef is a significant source of many nutrients that are essential to good health, and it fits the basics of healthy eating—balance, variety and moderation.

Because beef has a high level of nutrients as compared to calories, it is described as a *nutrient dense* food. Beef is one of the best sources of iron, the single nutrient most often lacking in the diets of adult women, young children and athletes. It contains a high percentage of heme iron, which is more easily absorbed by the body and five to ten times more available than nonheme iron from plant sources. It also has a special quality, called the *meat factor*, which helps the body utilize nonheme iron from other food sources.

Beef is also a major source of zinc, a mineral that is essential for growth and metabolism, and like iron often falls short in diets of women, children and athletes. It is especially difficult to obtain recommended amounts of zinc and iron when meat is not in the diet.

The protein in beef is nutritionally complete. It contains all the essential amino acids necessary for growth. Beef also is a major source of five of the B-complex vitamins, including thiamin, riboflavin, niacin and vitamins B-12 and B-6. Vitamin B-12, essential for growth and the synthesis of DNA, is only found naturally in animal foods.

An average three-ounce portion of cooked, trimmed lean beef provides 18% of niacin, 37% of vitamin B-12, 14% of iron and 39% of the zinc, as recommended in the U.S. RDA [recommended daily allowance]. And all for only 183 calories, or less than 10% of a 2000 calorie-per-day diet. Beef is truly a nutritional bargain.

Beef as Part of a Healthy Diet

Beef's role in a balanced and varied diet has been confirmed by leading health organizations. Most nutritionists agree that selections from the basic food groups, such as fruits, vegetables, cereals and grains, dairy products and meats, are an excellent foundation for a healthy diet.

Additionally, the *Dietary Guidelines* from the United States Department of Agriculture (USDA) and the Department of Health and Human Services promote the importance of eating a balanced and varied diet. The seven guidelines, used in partnership with the food groupings, will help you shape a healthful diet and select and prepare healthy foods for your family.

Table 1
Fat Content of Selected Protein Foods

Per 3-ounce cooked serving	Total Fat (grams)	Saturated Fatty Acids (grams)
Ground Beef 85% lean, broiled	12.2	4.8
Roasting Chicken w/skin, roasted	11.4	3.2
Pork Top Loin Chop boneless, trimmed, broiled	6.6	2.3
Beef Sirloin trimmed, broiled	6.1	2.4
Beef Top Round trimmed, broiled	4.2	1.4
Chicken Breast skinless, roasted	3.0	.9

Table 2
Cholesterol Content of Various Meats

Per 3-ounce cooked, trimmed serving	Cholesterol (milligrams)
Lamb	78
Broiler chicken, skinless, roasted	76
Beef, Lean	73
Pork, Lean	72
Turkey, white and dark, skinless	65
Flatfish (ie: flounder/sole)	58

Beef Industry Council, *Facts About Beef*, 1991.

The first two guidelines form the framework for a good diet:
- Eat a variety of foods
- Maintain healthy weight

The remaining five guidelines suggest specific strategies:
- Choose a diet low in fat, saturated fat and cholesterol
- Choose a diet with plenty of vegetables, fruits and grain products
- Use sugars only in moderation

- Use salt and sodium only in moderation
- If you drink alcoholic beverages, do so in moderation

More Beef Facts

The National Beef Market Basket Survey, conducted in 1987, showed that the beef sold at retail has 27% less trimmable fat than previously documented. The survey found that at retail the average thickness of fat around the edge of steaks and roasts was less than ⅛ inch, with over 40% of the cuts having no external fat at all.

Data from the survey provided information for updating the 1990 edition of the USDA's Agriculture Handbook 8-13. The handbook now has data on retail cuts with ¼ and 0-inch external fat and provides the most up-to-date nutritional information on beef.

According to the government data, an average three-ounce serving of today's cooked, trimmed lean beef contains only 8.4 grams of fat. The level of fat in selected protein foods is shown in Table 1.

Beef contains less dietary cholesterol than most people believe. In fact, an average three-ounce cooked, trimmed serving of lean beef has slightly less cholesterol than a three-ounce portion of roasted boneless, skinless chicken.

Beef has 73 milligrams of cholesterol, while chicken has 76 milligrams. (See Table 2.) Both fit well within the recommendation of no more than 300 mg of dietary cholesterol per day.

Although dietary saturated fatty acids are considered to play a more important role than dietary cholesterol in raising serum cholesterol, it's important to know that only 39% of beef fat is made up of saturated fatty acids. . . .

Beef, eaten in moderation, can be a valuable part of a balanced and varied diet.

> "Vegetarian diets reduce blood pressure in both healthy and hypertensive people."

Eating Meat Is Unhealthy

Neal D. Barnard

Neal D. Barnard is a well-known physician who writes often on health issues. He is the president of the Physicians Committee for Responsible Medicine, a Washington, D.C.-based organization that promotes good health and nutrition. In the following viewpoint, Barnard criticizes the food pyramid that replaced the old "four basic food groups" model for good nutrition in 1990. Barnard maintains that although the pyramid's emphasis on fruits, vegetables, and grains is an improvement, it still recommends two to three servings of meat and dairy products every day. Meat consumption, Barnard argues, is responsible for many of the major health problems that plague the United States.

As you read, consider the following questions:

1. Which industry lobbying groups affect the *Dietary Guidelines for Americans*, according to the author?
2. What are the chronic health problems in the United States that Barnard relates to meat consumption?
3. How does the author propose to change the dietary guidelines?

Neal D. Barnard, "The Pyramid Crumbles," *Good Medicine*, Summer 1995. Reprinted by permission of the author.

Every five years, the government revises the *Dietary Guidelines for Americans*—the nation's blueprint for nutrition programs. And when it does, it hears from the National Cattlemen's Association, the Chocolate Manufacturer's Association, the National Dairy Council, the Salt Institute, the Sugar Association, the United Egg Producers, and other industry groups on how their products should fit into the government's recommendations. The food lobby has made sure that the *Dietary Guidelines* read as much like a fast-food menu as a scientific document, catering to America's dietary habits as much as guiding them.

Eating Meat Causes Chronic Illness

Although countries whose diets are plant-centered—based on rice, pasta, or other plant products—have phenomenally low rates of chronic illness, U.S. nutrition guidelines have continued to promote daily meat and dairy product consumption. The result is continuing epidemics of heart disease, cancer, and other serious illnesses.

Obesity is so common that, at any point in time, one in three women and one in four men is dieting. Diabetes, hypertension, and other chronic illnesses take not only a terrible personal toll, but a mushrooming financial toll as well. As much as $60 billion of our annual direct health care costs and hundreds of billions in indirect costs are due to the diseases caused by the fat- and cholesterol-laden American diet.

When the Dietary Guidelines Advisory Committee met in March 1995 to consider changes to the *Dietary Guidelines*, it heard a remarkable new voice. Leading physicians and scientists from across the United States joined PCRM in calling for a massive redrawing of basic diet policies. Among them were Dr. Benjamin Spock, the author of *Baby and Child Care*, which has long been the leading guide for parents; Dr. Henry Heimlich, the inventor of the Heimlich Maneuver and many other medical innovations; Dr. William Castelli, Director of the Framingham Heart Study; Dr. William Roberts, the Editor of the *American Journal of Cardiology*; Dr. Dean Ornish, from the University of California at San Francisco; Dr. Peter Wood, of the Stanford Center for Research in Disease Prevention; Dr. Caldwell Esselstyn, Jr., of the Cleveland Clinic's Department of General Surgery; Dr. Frank Oski, Chairman of the Department of Pediatrics at Johns Hopkins University; Dr. Lawrence Kushi, of the University of Minnesota; Dr. Oliver Alabaster, the Director of the Institute for Disease Prevention of the George Washington University Medical Center; and many others.

This distinguished group called for the meat- and dairy-based diet to be traded for a plant-based diet. Recommended foods are grains, vegetables, fruits, and legumes—and the pasta, bean burritos, veggie chilies, and other foods that come from them.

The Food Guide Pyramid, which was unveiled in 1990, also needs to be redrawn. While it suggests that grains, vegetables, and fruits should be emphasized in the diet, it still recommends 2–3 servings of meat and 2–3 servings of dairy products every day, which flies in the face of research showing that avoiding such products is safer than consuming them.

Dietary Guidelines

Here are the seven current *Dietary Guidelines for Americans,* and a summary of our recommended changes.

Guideline 1: Eat a Variety of Foods

The recommendation for variety should be in the context of plant foods only. Meats and dairy products should be optional rather than recommended.

Health Benefits of a Vegetarian Diet

The consumption of animal products has been conclusively linked with heart disease, cancer, diabetes, arthritis, and osteoporosis. Cholesterol (found only in animal products) and animal fat clog arteries, leading to heart attacks and strokes. A vegetarian diet can prevent 97 percent of coronary occlusions. The rate of colon cancer is highest in regions where meat consumption is high, and lowest where meat-eating is uncommon. A similar pattern is evident for breast, cervical, uterine, ovarian, prostate, and lung cancers.

Low-fat diets, particularly those without saturated fat, have been instrumental in allowing many diabetics to dispense with their pills, shots, and pumps. A study of more than 25,000 people over age 21 found that vegetarians have a much lower risk of getting diabetes than meat-eaters.

A South African study found not a single case of rheumatoid arthritis in a community of 800 people who ate no meat or dairy products. Another study found that a similar group that ate meat and other high-fat foods had almost four times the incidence of arthritis as those on a low-fat diet.

People for the Ethical Treatment of Animals, "Vegetarianism: Eating for Life," June 1995.

Guideline 2: Maintain a Healthy Weight

The emphasis should be shifting from a fatty diet to a high-carbohydrate, plant-based diet, not on reducing calorie intake. Carbohydrate-rich foods (e.g. grains, beans, and vegetables) are naturally modest in calories, lose 23 percent of their calorie content in the process of conversion to fat, and increase body metabolism so calories are burned more quickly. Most animal products are much higher in fat than typical vegetables, fruits, grains, or legumes, and they contain no complex carbohydrate or fiber.

Guideline 3: Choose a Diet Low in Fat, Saturated Fat, and Cholesterol

Not all consumers will know where fat, saturated fat, and cholesterol are found. Rather than describe nutrients, this guideline should describe specific foods. Cholesterol is found only in animal products. The main sources of fat and saturated fat are animal products, added vegetable oils, fried foods, and some baked goods.

Guideline 4: Choose a Diet with Plenty of Vegetables, Fruits, and Grain Products

This section merits increased emphasis. Vegetables, fruits, grains, and beans differ in their nutrient profiles and should be separated to emphasize the importance of each of these groups.

Guideline 5: Use Sugars Only in Moderation

This guideline is helpful, but of secondary importance.

Guideline 6: Use Salt and Sodium Only in Moderation

This guideline is useful, but incomplete. First, it suggests that hypertension is the only problem caused by excessive sodium intake. However, calcium loss and an increased risk of osteoporosis are also important effects of high sodium intake.

Second, salt is not the only factor that influences blood pressure. The fat content of the diet influences blood pressure, and vegetarian diets reduce blood pressure in both healthy and hypertensive people.

The highest-sodium products are canned goods prepared with added salt and snack foods. Animal products are higher in sodium than plant foods, unless salt is added.

Guideline 7: If You Drink Alcoholic Beverages, Do So in Moderation

The link between alcohol and breast cancer should be mentioned. The elevated risk is found even when the one drink per day limit currently prescribed for women is followed.

Risks of other beverage ingredients should also be noted. Caffeine contributes to calcium loss from bones, a factor which should be better publicized. Otherwise, consumers may imagine that bone strength depends on dairy product consumption, a dangerously inaccurate notion.

"The scientific case against milk consumption grows stronger by the day."

Milk Consumption Is Harmful

Nathaniel Mead

It has long been thought that cow's milk contributes to good health. In the following viewpoint, Nathaniel Mead argues that the reported health benefits from milk have mostly been advertising fiction and that milk consumption leads to health problems that include asthma, allergies, appendicitis, and ovarian cancer. Mead, a former dairy farmer, is the author of *Udder Nonsense: Why Milk Is No Longer Required or Recommended*.

As you read, consider the following questions:

1. Why have advertisers been so successful in promoting milk consumption, according to the author?
2. What harmful effects do dairy products have on children, according to Mead?
3. What factors does Mead cite that determine whether or not milk will become a health problem?

Nathaniel Mead, "Don't Drink Your Milk," *Natural Health*, July/August 1994. Reprinted with permission. For a trial issue of *Natural Health*, call 1-800-526-8440.

Asked what single change in the American diet would produce the greatest health benefit, Washington, D.C.–based pediatrician Russell Bunai says, "Eliminating dairy products." Bunai has observed the effects of cow's milk on the health of children and their families for more than two decades. In the 1960s, when he served as a missionary in Ghana, West Africa, Bunai noticed that certain diseases prevalent in areas where people ate dairy were absent in areas free of dairy consumption.

"At first I noticed that where people consumed milk products, asthma and allergic conditions were common. In contrast, I rarely saw asthma, hives, or other allergies in areas free from dairy consumption. Gradually it became clear that arthritis, appendicitis, and inflammatory bowel disease followed a similar pattern. Over the years, the list of diseases associated with dairy continued to lengthen."

Bunai is not alone in believing that our health would be improved if we cut out dairy. Increasing numbers of researchers, physicians, nutritionists, and other health professionals have begun to see milk as a food we could do without. (References to milk and dairy products in this article are to cow's milk; there are far fewer studies of the milks of other animals.)

We were raised to think of cow's milk as the perfect food. The National Dairy Council advertises that "milk is a natural" and "you never outgrow your need for milk." If you don't drink milk, the Council warns, your bones will become brittle and your strength will fade. Partly out of fear, many Americans make dairy products a staple of their diets.

Milk is also an easy sell. "We are moved from mother's milk to cow's milk very early [in life], so that the taste of cow's milk is associated with being held next to mother's breast," said Steven Locke, instructor in psychiatry and director of the psychoimmunology research project at Harvard Medical School, in a 1988 interview with the *New York Times*. "Milk has a bigger-than-life image because it's [linked] to mothering in ways that only Madison Avenue could appreciate."

But the scientific case against milk consumption grows stronger by the day. Most of the publicity about milk's dangers has focused on its fat content, which is a real concern. Fat is a known contributing factor in heart disease and has been associated with cancers of the mouth, stomach, colon, rectum, cervix, bladder, lung, and breast. While the problems with milk fat are reduced by substituting low-fat or skim milk for whole milk, other serious problems remain.

Scientists have found numerous reasons to be wary of dairy, including the following:

Galactose. Ovarian cancer rates parallel dairy-eating patterns around the world. The culprit seems to be galactose, the simple sugar broken down from the milk sugar lactose. Animals fed galactose go on to develop ovarian cancer. According to Boston gynecologist Daniel Cramer, women with this cancer often have trouble breaking down galactose. "About 10 percent of the U.S. population lacks the enzymes to metabolize galactose," says Cramer. "Since you can't tell whether you lack these enzymes

Casting Dairy in a Minor Role

Many Americans consume dairy in order to get enough calcium, too little of which is believed to cause osteoporosis, the "brittle-bone" condition that occurs in older people. . . .

If you eat plenty of green vegetables and possibly sea vegetables (all high in calcium), reduce your overall consumption of animal protein, and exercise outdoors on a regular basis, then you likely can cast dairy into a minor role in your diet, if not eliminate it altogether.

Counting on Calcium

1 cup cow's milk — 288 mg

1 cup cooked collard greens — 290 mg

1 cup cooked bok choy — 250 mg

3.5 oz. corn tortilla (lime treated) — 300 mg

4 oz. cooked tofu — 154 mg

1 cup cooked kale — 148 mg

1/2 cup cooked hijiki seaweed — 306 mg

3 oz. sardines (with bones) — 372 mg

Nathaniel Mead, *Natural Health*, July/August 1994.

[unlike lactose intolerance, in which there are clear signs of digestive upset], I just tell my patients they don't need dairy." Yogurt, cheese, and other fermented dairy products, as well as those containing Lactaid, are the richest sources of galactose.

Pesticides. Pesticides concentrate in milk of both farm animals and humans. A study by the Environmental Defense Fund found widespread pesticide contamination of human breast milk among 1,400 women in forty-six states. The levels of contamination were twice as high among the meat- and dairy-eating women as among vegetarians.

Antibiotic-Resistant Bacteria. Joseph Beasley, M.D., and Jerry Swift wrote in *The Kellogg Report* (The Institute of Health Policy and Practice, 1989) that even "moderate use of antibiotics in animal feed can result in the development of antibiotic resistance in animal bacteria—and the subsequent transfer of that resistance to human bacteria." According to an August 1992 report in *Science*, "[D]octors . . . around the world are losing the battle against an onslaught of new drug-resistant bacterial infections including staph, pneumonia, strep, tuberculosis, dysentery, and other diseases."

Vitamin D Toxicity. Heavy consumption of milk, especially by small children, may result in vitamin D toxicity. Records show that dairies do not carefully regulate how much vitamin D is added to milk. (Milk has been "fortified" with vitamin D ever since deficiencies were found to cause rickets, even though the vitamin is easily obtained through minimal exposure to sunlight.) A study reported in the *New England Journal of Medicine* showed that of forty-two milk samples, only 12 percent were within the expected range of vitamin D content. Testing of ten infant formula samples revealed seven with more than twice the vitamin D content reported on the label; one sample had more than four times the label amount.

Growth hormones. Recently, cows have started to receive growth hormones to increase their milk production, although the long-term effects on humans are unknown. The General Accounting Office says the hormone, bovine somatotropin, or BST, increases the risk of mastitis, an udder disease that must be treated with antibiotics.

Don't Cry over Spilled Milk

Perhaps the biggest health problem with cow's milk arises from the proteins in it: Cow's milk proteins damage the human immune system. Amino acids, the units that make up proteins, are building blocks for all living cells. When protein in our food is properly broken down by the digestive system into amino acids, it does no harm to the immune system. Some food proteins, however, are absorbed into the blood fully undigested, provoking an immune response. Repeated exposure to these proteins disrupts normal immune function and may eventually lead to disease.

Cow's milk contains many proteins that are poorly digested and harmful to the immune system. Fish and meat proteins are much less damaging, while plant proteins pose the least hazard. "When we lose our wellness," Bunai says, "it is most often due to immune system damage and dysfunction. Most nutritionists and physicians focus only on the quantity of protein taken in, and ignore the pathogenic characteristics of the protein."

Removing dairy from the diet has been shown to shrink enlarged tonsils and adenoids, indicating relief for the immune system. Similarly, doctors experimenting with dairy-free diets often report a marked reduction in colds, flus, sinusitis, and ear infections.

"Dairy is a tremendous mucus producer and a burden on the respiratory, digestive, and immune systems," says Christiane Northrup, a gynecologist based in Yarmouth, Maine. "If women eliminate dairy foods for an extended period and eat a balanced diet, they suffer less from colds and sinus infections." In fact, the list of health problems attributed to the immune-damaging, or antigenic, properties of dairy goes on:

Colic and Ear Infections. One out of every five infants in the United States suffers bouts of colic. The colicky infant has severe belly cramps. When a mother eats dairy products, milk proteins pass into her breast milk and end up in the baby's blood; some studies have found that cow's milk proteins (from milk drunk by the mother) might trigger coliclike symptoms in infants fed only human milk and no cow's milk. Another common problem among infants receiving dairy, either directly or indirectly, is chronic ear infections. "You just don't see this painful condition among infants and children who aren't getting cow's milk into their systems," Northrup says.

Allergies, Asthma, and Sinus Problems. Poorly digested bovine antigens (substances that provoke an immune reaction) like casein become "allergens" in allergic individuals. Physician Frank A. Oski, author of *Don't Drink Your Milk* and chief of pediatrics at Johns Hopkins School of Medicine, cites evidence that at least 50 percent of all children in the United States are allergic to cow's milk, many undiagnosed. Dairy products are the leading cause of food allergy, often revealed by diarrhea, constipation, and fatigue. Many cases of asthma and sinus infections are reported to be relieved and even eliminated by cutting out dairy. The exclusion of dairy, however, must be complete to see any benefit.

Arthritis. Antigens in cow's milk may also contribute to rheumatoid arthritis and osteoarthritis. When antibody-antigen complexes (resulting from an immune response) are deposited in the joints, pain, swelling, redness, and stiffness result; these complexes increase in arthritic people who eat dairy products, and the pain fades rapidly after patients eliminate dairy products from their diets. In a study published in *Scandinavian Journal of Rheumatology*, when people with rheumatoid arthritis fasted on water, fruit and vegetable juices, and tea for seven to ten days, their joint pain and stiffness were greatly reduced. When they ate a lacto-ovo-vegetarian diet (including only milk and eggs as animal foods), the symptoms became aggravated and they remained ill.

Diabetes and Autoimmune Diseases. Consumption of cow's milk has been associated with insulin-dependent diabetes. The milk protein bovine serum albumin (BSA) somehow leads to an autoimmune reaction aimed at the pancreas and ultimately to impairment of the pancreas's ability to produce insulin. According to a 1992 report in the *New England Journal of Medicine*, all of 142 diabetic children studied had abnormally high levels of BSA antibodies. This research suggests that a combination of genetic predisposition and exposure to cow's milk leads to juvenile diabetes.

Childhood Anemia. Cow's milk causes loss of iron and hemoglobin in infants (one reason the American Academy of Pediatrics recommends that infants not drink cow's milk) by triggering blood loss from the intestinal tract. Some research also shows that iron absorption is blocked by as much as 60 percent when dairy products are consumed in the same meal.

Non-Hodgkin's Lymphoma and Lung Cancer. A 1989 study in *Nutrition and Cancer* linked the risk of developing non-Hodgkin's lymphoma with the consumption of cow's milk and butter. A growing consensus among scientists is that animal proteins, particularly dairy proteins, play a major role in the genesis of this cancer of the immune system. High levels of the cow's milk protein beta-lactoglobulin have also been found in the blood of lung cancer patients, suggesting a link with this cancer as well.

The Bottom Line

People in different parts of the world eat varying amounts of dairy food. What determines whether it becomes a health-negating food seems to depend on two things: your innate resistance (how well your body can cope with the proteins, fats, sugars, and chemicals) and how much of it you consume. There is a big difference between consuming large amounts of milk, cheese, and ice cream and adding a teaspoon or so of milk to your morning beverage or a few tablespoons of yogurt to your fruit.

However, if you or anyone in your family is experiencing health problems of almost any kind and dairy is a part of your diet, it makes sense to completely eliminate the dairy for at least a month and observe the results. It would not surprise Bunai and others if you found relief.

"Milk and dairy products are safe and nutritious foods for growing children."

The Health Risks of Milk Consumption Are Exaggerated

Kathleen Meister

In the following viewpoint, Kathleen Meister refutes the charge that milk universally causes health problems. She notes that while cow's milk should not be fed to infants, it is an important part of a well-balanced diet for children and adults. Meister concedes that some individuals need to restrict their dairy intake to prevent certain health problems, but she insists that eliminating dairy products completely would only promote other serious health and nutrition problems. Meister is a freelance writer and the associate editor of *Nutrition Research Newsletter*.

As you read, consider the following questions:

1. How does Meister counter the contention that milk causes iron-deficiency anemia?
2. Members of what racial groups develop gastrointestinal problems as a result of drinking substantial amounts of milk, according to the author?
3. What conclusions can be drawn from studies of the relationship between milk and diabetes, according to Meister?

Excerpted from Kathleen Meister, "Much Ado About Milk," *Priorities*, Spring 1993. Reprinted by permission of the American Council on Science and Health.

Controversy about nutrition seems a constant in the news. Yet in September 1992, the surprising target was milk. An organization called the Physicians Committee for Responsible Medicine held a press conference in which they claimed that cows' milk is hazardous to children's health, that parents should be warned of its dangers and that it should not be required or recommended in government guidelines. The Committee charged that cows' milk is harmful to health in a wide variety of ways. Let's look closely at these allegations to see if they are justified.

The Allegations

Cows' milk should not be fed to infants This is true, but it is certainly not news. Experts have long known that unmodified cows' milk is unsuitable for infants in the first six months of life because its composition is too different from that of human breast milk. Recognized authorities, including the American Academy of Pediatrics, also recommend that unmodified cows' milk not be fed in the second six months of life. At this age, iron deficiency is the main concern. Cows' milk is low in iron, and the other foods commonly consumed by infants don't make up the difference. Also, unmodified cows' milk causes some babies to lose small but significant amounts of blood in their stool; important amounts of iron can be lost in this way. Breast milk is clearly the best milk throughout the first year of life, and iron-fortified infant formula is the only acceptable alternative.

Cows' milk causes iron-deficiency anemia It can, in infants, but infants shouldn't be drinking it. If they are not nursing, they should be drinking iron-fortified formula. The most commonly used formulas are made from cows' milk, but they contain added iron and they receive a heat treatment sufficient to inactivate the agent that causes intestinal blood loss.

An older child could become iron-deficient if he or she drinks too much milk and doesn't eat enough iron-rich foods. In such a case, the child obviously needs a better-balanced diet. The problem should not be "solved" by eliminating milk from the child's diet—that would just replace one type of dietary imbalance with another.

Cows' milk is a common cause of allergy Actually, food allergies in general are much less common than people believe. It is true, however, that when a real food allergy is diagnosed, cows' milk is a likely culprit. The small number of children who are actually allergic to cows' milk should avoid it in any form. However, there is no need for the rest of the population to avoid drinking milk just because a few people are allergic.

Dairy products are high in fat and cholesterol. Therefore they cause heart disease Actually, people who are concerned about fat and cholesterol do not need to avoid dairy products. They simply need to choose them carefully. Skim or 1 percent lowfat milk is perfectly acceptable for a person on a cholesterol-lowering diet. Lowfat or nonfat yogurts and cheeses are also good choices. A reduced-fat diet need not be dairy-free.

No Miracle Foods

In reality, there is no such thing as a miracle food or food ingredient. There are no "bad" or "good" foods. All food products contain nutrients that the body needs. Eating a variety of foods in moderate amounts ensures good nutrition, just as sure as overdosing on broccoli or eliminating milk or beef can be harmful. The ingredients of a healthy diet can be found in abundance in every supermarket aisle.

Andrea Golaine Case, *Priorities*, Spring 1993.

Dairy products cause digestive problems Some Americans, especially those of African or Asian heritage, develop gastrointestinal symptoms when they drink substantial amounts of milk. These symptoms are caused by the inability to digest lactose, the sugar found in milk.

Lactose-intolerant people do not need to eliminate all dairy products from their diets; they simply need to choose them carefully. Commercial lactose-reduced milk is available in many areas. Consumers can also buy enzyme drops in pharmacies and use them to treat milk at home. Hard cheeses, such as cheddar, Swiss and American, contain almost no lactose. Yogurt is also a good choice; the bacteria in yogurt culture digest lactose during passage through the digestive tract. Some lactose-intolerant people can even drink regular milk, as long as they limit the amount that they consume at any one time. The idea is to keep lactose intake down to a level that does not cause discomfort; the limit differs for different individuals.

Milk and Diabetes

Cows' milk causes diabetes This is the big one—the most frightening of the allegations made by the Physicians Committee for Responsible Medicine. It is based on an overzealous interpretation of some very preliminary scientific evidence.

Scientists have suspected for years that early exposure to cows' milk proteins might be one of the factors that can trigger the onset of Type 1 diabetes mellitus in susceptible people. Type 1 diabetes is a severe form of the disease that usually begins in childhood or young adulthood. It has a strong hereditary component and, unlike the more common Type 2 diabetes that begins

33

in later adulthood, it is not associated with obesity.

Some people who inherit the genetic predisposition to Type 1 diabetes develop the disease; others do not. Environmental factors may play a role in triggering the onset of clinical illness. Cows' milk proteins may be one of those factors because they increase the rate of disease in some animal models of Type 1 diabetes. Laboratory animals, however, do not always react in the same way that humans do, and experimentally induced model diseases can have important differences from the real thing.

Some studies of human populations have associated longer duration of breast feeding and/or delayed introduction of cows' milk into an infant's diet with lower risks of Type 1 diabetes. Other studies, however, have not confirmed these associations. There have even been cases of Type 1 diabetes in children who were never exposed to cows' milk in any form.

A much-publicized study released in the summer of 1992 showed that patients who had just been diagnosed with Type 1 diabetes had high levels of an antibody to a particular cows' milk protein; healthy individuals had much lower levels. Despite the furor generated by this finding, no one really knows what it means. The high antibody levels may be a result rather than a cause of the metabolic derangement that occurs at the onset of diabetes.

Because this evidence is so preliminary and so poorly understood, all recognized authorities agree that it does not justify any recommendation for dietary modifications—not even in infants with a family history of Type 1 diabetes. The American Academy of Pediatrics, in particular, has taken strong exception to the Physicians Committee for Responsible Medicine's stance on this issue. A spokesperson for the Academy accused the group of "practicing nutritional terrorism" by frightening American parents on the basis of such tentative scientific findings.

A Regulated Product

Cows' milk contains dangerous contaminants Actually, cows' milk is one of the most regulated commodities sold in the U.S. It rarely contains even detectable amounts of pesticide residues or animal drugs, let alone much larger amounts that could cause illness. However, one significant contamination problem has recently come to light—overfortification with vitamin D.

Vitamin D fortification of milk has played a crucial role in the near-elimination of the deficiency disease rickets in the U.S. It is essential, however, that fortification be carried out correctly. Excessive amounts of vitamin D can cause serious toxicity problems.

Studies published in 1992 showed that milk sold in the U.S. is sometimes underfortified or overfortified with vitamin D. In one instance, involving a Massachusetts dairy, extreme overfortification led to several cases of illness. Clearly, there is a need for better control of the fortification process. The necessary regulations already exist, but they should be enforced more strictly.

Health and nutrition authorities have urged that the policy of fortifying milk with vitamin D should not be abandoned; rickets is still a potential problem, especially in northern latitudes, where sunlight may not provide enough vitamin D. It would be even more unwise to eliminate the consumption of milk in order to avoid vitamin D toxicity.

Drinking cows' milk is unnatural; humans are the only creatures who drink the milk of another species Well, yes, this is true. But the proponents of this argument don't seem to realize that practically everything else that we eat and drink is just as unnatural as milk.

On an evolutionary time scale, dairying is indeed a very recent invention. So is the milling of grains. Grains are the staple food for most people today, but until 15,000 years ago, our ancestors didn't eat them because they didn't know how to mill them. They didn't eat poultry or fish either until about 20,000 years ago. They did eat red meats and vegetables, but the variety and composition were very different from those of the meats and vegetables that we consume today. It is impossible to return to the diet that was "natural" for the human species; agriculture has transformed the world's food supply.

People don't need to drink milk. It's easy to get plenty of calcium from other food sources It is possible to get enough calcium, but it's far from easy. Dairy products are the principal source of calcium in the U.S. diet, and most of the other foods that Americans prefer are not rich in this mineral. Getting enough calcium from a dairy-free diet requires the use of large amounts of foods not favored by most American children, such as fish with edible bones, leafy green vegetables, broccoli, tofu and legumes. (It takes roughly one cup of legumes plus one cup of leafy greens to supply as much calcium as a glass of milk.) Even the Physicians Committee for Responsible Medicine doesn't find it easy to plan a dairy-free diet with adequate calcium content. In two of the three sample menus included in their literature, they resort to artificially fortified foods (fortified soy milk and calcium-fortified orange juice) to provide a substantial portion of the day's calcium supply.

A Safe and Nutritious Food

Of course, cows' milk is not a perfect food. It doesn't need to be. No single food can meet all nutrient needs or be suitable for unlimited consumption by everyone. Some people, especially those who must limit their intakes of fat or lactose, must choose dairy products carefully. The few people with true cows' milk allergies must avoid dairy products. Infants under one year should not drink unmodified cows' milk.

There is no scientific justification, however, for the Physicians Committee for Responsible Medicine's campaign to eliminate cows' milk from the American diet. As Dr. Ronald E. Kleinman of the American Academy of Pediatrics stated, in response to the Committee's allegations, "Milk and dairy products are safe and nutritious foods for growing children, and parents should make use of them unless there's some specific medical reason to avoid them. . . . Dairy products are not perfect foods, but they are concentrated with many of the forms of nutrients that children need to grow well."

"Mere vitamins may have the power to cut some common birth defects by half, protect the elderly from bone loss and hip fractures, and dramatically reduce the incidence of heart disease."

Vitamin Supplements Are Beneficial

Geoffrey Cowley

While relatively few Americans suffer from acute vitamin deficiencies, Geoffrey Cowley contends, significantly increasing vitamin intake may prevent a host of serious illnesses. In the following viewpoint, the author maintains that as scientists learn more about the importance of certain vitamins and minerals in warding off heart disease, cancer, birth defects, and other health problems, new importance may be placed on vitamin supplements. Cowley is on the staff of *Newsweek*, a weekly journal of news and information.

As you read, consider the following questions:

1. How does the author describe the old attitude of the medical community toward vitamins?
2. According to the author, what are vitamins?
3. What role do scientists think free radicals play in fomenting disease, according to Cowley?

Jerome Cohen, M.D., is no faddist. A professor of internal medicine at the St. Louis University School of Medicine, he used to dismiss the notion that healthy adults had anything to gain from vitamin pills. Not anymore. In an effort to keep his heart healthy, Cohen now starts the day with 400 international units of vitamin E—roughly the amount he would get in 25 cups of peanuts. Though he isn't sure the new regimen will do him any good, he's now happy to wager a couple of bucks a month on it. Dr. Stephen Deutsch, the head of a 40-doctor medical practice in Beverly Hills, Calif., has had a similar conversion. "I used to be very anti-vitamin," he says. "I didn't tell people they couldn't take them, but I certainly didn't push them." Today Deutsch urges patients not only to eat well and exercise but to take a little C, E and beta carotene every day.

Cohen and Deutsch may be a step ahead of their colleagues, but their stories reflect a fundamental shift in the way the medical world views vitamins. "Until quite recently, it was taught that everyone in this country gets enough vitamins through their diet and that taking supplements just creates expensive urine," says Dr. Walter Willett, a Harvard epidemiologist studying diet, supplements and chronic diseases. "I think we have proof that this isn't true. I think the scientific community has realized this is a very important area for research."

Higher Vitamin Intakes

That's an understatement. A growing body of evidence suggests that while the old daily allowances are fine for warding off acute deficiencies, higher intakes may help combat everything from bone loss to cancer. Willett and his colleagues grabbed the world's attention with two new studies suggesting that vitamin E can help prevent heart disease, the nation's leading killer. The researchers followed more than 120,000 men and women for up to eight years and found that those taking daily supplements of at least 100 units reduced their risk of heart disease by about 40 percent. Other recent studies have shown that B vitamins can prevent birth defects. And some scientists now believe that vitamin D could become a vital tool for preventing breast cancer.

Major research organizations are launching efforts to tap vitamins' full potential. Many of the brightest prospects will take years to confirm, but consumers aren't waiting idly. A *News-week* poll shows that 7 in 10 Americans use vitamin supplements at least occasionally, and 15 percent of daily users say they have started in the past year. As the market for vitamins and other food supplements explodes, health officials worry that consumers are more vulnerable than ever to phony health claims. But if even half of today's promising leads pan out, they could change our whole approach to nutrition. "There's very solid data to suggest that nutrients can promote optimal health and prevent chronic disease," says Dr. Jeffrey Blumberg of Tufts University's Center for the Study of Human Nutrition and Aging. "This is a new paradigm."

Vitamins Are Chemicals

Vitamins are simply chemicals that our bodies use in tiny amounts to build, maintain and repair tissues. The first ones were identified in the early part of this century, after researchers found that eating certain foods protected people from diseases like rickets, pellagra and beriberi, which had once been deemed infectious. The acute-deficiency diseases were largely eradicated during the 1930s, as chemists learned to synthesize various vitamins and food manufacturers started adding them to milk, flour and rice. By 1941, the National Academy of Science's Food and Nutrition Board was publishing recommended daily allowances (RDAs) for most of the 13 vitamins.

The RDAs are periodically updated, but they still reflect the old thinking, and they've begun to show their age. In the case of folic acid, many experts consider the RDAs woefully obsolete. Folic acid, a B vitamin found in yeast, liver and leafy green vegetables, aids in various metabolic processes, including the synthesis of DNA. When a shortage of folic acid interferes with that process, the body may produce aberrant cells. The official guidelines recommend a daily intake of 180 to 200 micrograms to prevent anemia, but recent research suggests that women of childbearing age need higher doses to help prevent certain birth defects. Studies have suggested that women need 400 to 800 micrograms a day during the first six weeks of pregnancy to ensure proper development of a fetus's neural tube, the tissue that becomes the brain and spinal cord. Lower intakes have been linked to neural-tube defects such as anencephaly (which causes death just hours after delivery) and spina bifida (which can cause everything from paralysis to lifelong bowel and bladder problems). The Food and Nutrition Board does provide a separate RDA of 400 micrograms for women who are pregnant. The trouble is, most women don't even learn they're pregnant until the critical six weeks have passed. Despite the RDA, the U.S. Public Health Service now advises all women of childbearing age to take 400 micrograms daily.

The Benefits of Folic Acid

Pregnancy isn't the only reason women may need extra folic acid. Researchers at the University of Alabama found that among women infected with HPV-16, a virus implicated in cervical cancer, those with the highest levels of folic acid in their blood were the least likely to exhibit precancerous lesions. In an

Vitamins and Minerals

Vitamins

	Food Sources	Benefits/Risks
Beta Carotene	Beta carotene is common in fruits such as cantaloupe and peaches and vegetables such as broccoli.	*Benefits:* When converted into vitamin A, it helps the eyes and the immune system. Also associated with lower risks for some cancers. *Risks:* Nontoxic, because the body's own systems convert it into vitamin A only as needed.
Vitamin C RDA Women and men: 60 mg	Citrus fruits and brussels sprouts are the best bet, though strawberries and cantaloupe are also good sources.	*Benefits:* Vitamin C might reduce the tissue damage that causes cancer and accelerates aging. There are signs of increased resistance to colds. *Risks:* Massive daily doses—10,000 mg—can cause diarrhea and nausea.
Vitamin D RDA Women and men: 200 iu	One cup of vitamin-D-fortified milk provides 100 iu, and some breakfast cereals contain added vitamin D. The best source: canned sardines, which pack 1,100 iu in 3.5 oz.	*Benefits:* Vitamin D shows promise as an anticancer agent. It also seems to help weak immune systems and weak bones. *Risks:* Daily doses of 1,000 iu or more can cause heart problems.
Vitamin E RDA Women: 12 iu Men: 15 iu	Hard to get from standard diets, the richest natural sources of vitamin E are wheat germ, safflower and sunflower oils; smaller amounts are in foods like peaches and prunes.	*Benefits:* Large doses of this antioxidant may protect against heart disease and certain cancers. Studies show it could also help treat arthritis and some skin conditions. *Risks:* Safe at 100 times the RDA.

Minerals

Calcium RDA Women and men over 25: 800 mg	Yogurt, milk and cheese are classic calcium sources. Tofu and sardines also contain plenty; oysters, dried apricots and whole-wheat bread have smaller amounts.	*Benefits:* Calcium is essential for strong bones and teeth. Supplements can help aging women avoid osteoporosis. *Risks:* More than several grams per day can cause urinary stones and nausea.
Iron RDA Women: 15 mg Men: 10 mg	Liver, oysters and beef are good sources, as are dried apricots and black-strap molasses.	*Benefits:* Iron strengthens chemical links in the brain; iron-deficient children have trouble learning. Regulated doses help the immune system. *Risks:* Some studies have linked high iron levels to heart disease in adults.

Source: *Newsweek*, June 7, 1993.

earlier study, the same team showed that when heavy smokers took 1,000 micrograms of folic acid along with B_{12} supplements every day, they were less likely than untreated smokers to develop precancerous lung lesions. Since folic acid is usually safe at high levels, some experts now advise smokers to increase their intake, at least until they manage to quit.

Vitamin D, which largely eradicated rickets 50 years ago, is another old nutrient that's gaining new respect. Though it's found in some foods (mainly fish oils and fortified milk), our bodies manufacture it when exposed to sunlight and use it to ferry calcium from food into the blood and bones. People who drink a quart of milk a day get plenty of vitamin D (the RDAs are 400 units for children, 200 for grown-ups), but many adults fall short. The deficiencies may contribute to osteoporosis, the bone decay that disables millions of elderly people.

Frank and Cedric Garland, both epidemiologists at the University of California, San Diego, are leading a growing group of scientists who suspect that a lack of vitamin D also fosters breast, colon and prostate cancer. Virtually unknown at the equator, all three cancers become more and more prevalent at higher latitudes. It's clear from lab studies that vitamin D can retard the growth of cancer cells in test tubes and in animals. The Garlands have amassed voluminous evidence that colon-cancer rates vary according to people's sun exposure, the amount of vitamin D in their diets and the amount of vitamin D in their blood. They've recently shown that the same principle applies to breast cancer, a disease that more widely publicized risk factors such as fat intake have done little to explain. Other researchers have found that prostate cancer, an equally mysterious affliction, follows the same pattern. Clinical trials won't start to yield results for another decade or so. But if the Garlands are right, the battle against breast cancer may ultimately be won not with lasers or designer genes but with a little vitamin D added to ice cream, cottage cheese and yogurt.

Antioxidants and Free Radicals

For other chronic diseases, plain old fruits and vegetables may be the secret to prevention. The big stars of the vitamin craze are the so-called antioxidants: vitamins C and E, and beta carotene, a form of vitamin A with its own special properties. Since 1988 the U.S. market for beta carotene supplements has soared from $7 million to $82 million a year, while vitamin E sales have jumped from $260 million to $338 million. The reason can be summed up in two words: free radicals. These molecules, which crop up in our bodies with every breath we take, are implicated in some 60 age-related afflictions, including cancer and heart disease. Unlike a stable molecule, in which every atom is ringed by pairs of electrons, a free radical carries an unmatched electron with a strong impulse to mate. By snatching an electron from a neighbor, it can set off a chain reaction that wreaks widespread havoc on cells, eating away at their membranes and damaging their genetic material.

The body has elaborate strategies for controlling this corrosive process, known as oxidation, but the safeguards aren't foolproof. Countless stresses, from smoking to aging, can accelerate oxidative damage. That's where the antioxidant vitamins come in. Biochemists have long suspected that vitamin E, vitamin C and beta carotene can neutralize free radicals by binding their lonely electrons. The first hints that antioxidant vitamins might help prevent cancer came from surveys in the 1970s showing that incidence is lowest in populations where people consume the most fruits and vegetables. A review published by Dr. Gladys Block of the University of California, Berkeley, tallied the results of 20 studies that monitored the incidence of mouth, throat and stomach cancers in relation to vitamin C intake. In 18 of those 20 studies, low intake emerged as a clear risk factor: on average, people consuming the least vitamin C were stricken at twice the rate of those consuming the most.

Regina Ziegler, an epidemiologist at the National Cancer Institute, uncovered similar trends when she analyzed more than 20 studies that tracked cancers of the lung and other tissues in relation to beta carotene intake. Virtually all the studies linked high levels of the nutrient to low rates of lung cancer. The studies showed similar but less dramatic patterns for cancers of the mouth, throat, stomach, bladder and rectum. It's possible, of course, that something other than vitamin intake accounts for the variations these studies have documented. To prove cause and effect, scientists have put people on measured doses of particular vitamins and recorded the long-term effects. At least 12 such "chemoprevention" studies are under way. Health authorities have calculated that if antioxidants really explain all the variations seen in the population studies, simply getting people to consume more of them could reduce U.S. cancer mortality by a third.

Vitamins' Skeptics

Heart experts are notoriously skeptical of vitamin claims, but they, too, are embracing the antioxidant revolution—and with good reason. A decade of laboratory research has shown that oxidation is what makes cholesterol so harmful to coronary arteries, and there's growing evidence that antioxidants can help block the phenomenon.

Only a handful of human studies have been published, but most have pointed in the same direction as the vitamin E findings at Harvard. After analyzing results from a decadelong federal health survey, researchers at UCLA reported that low vitamin C intake was a strong predictor of death from heart disease and other causes. During the study, men who consumed in the neighborhood of 300 milligrams daily (five times the RDA) suffered 40 percent fewer deaths than those consuming less than 50 milligrams. Meanwhile, researchers at Harvard have found preliminary evidence that 50-milligram beta carotene supplements, taken every other day, can halve the risk of heart attack among men with histories of cardiovascular disease. Such findings are doubly encouraging because the antioxidants are so safe. Excessive vitamin C may cause diarrhea, but the body expels what it can't use, so overdose isn't a danger. Vitamin E and beta carotene can accumulate in our fat stores, but neither is known to cause any side effect more serious than a stomachache or a reversible yellowing of the skin.

As any doctor will tell you, the real secrets to good health are exercising, giving up cigarettes and substituting carrots for candy bars. Those measures alone could work much of the magic that millions of Americans now seek in vitamin pills. But there may be excellent reasons to take supplements as well. If today's hopes are realized, mere vitamins may have the power to cut some common birth defects by half, protect the elderly from bone loss and hip fractures, and dramatically reduce the incidence of heart disease and cancer. Best of all, this medical revolution won't require a new generation of weaponry. Your corner drugstore is already armed to the teeth.

"The scientific evidence to date does not provide a firm basis for advocating dietary supplementation in normal, healthy adults to prevent chronic diseases."

The Benefits of Vitamin Supplements Are Unproven

Ruth Kava

Ruth Kava is the director of nutrition for the American Council on Science and Health (ACSH), a New York–based organization that conducts health and science research and provides consumer information. In the following viewpoint, Kava asserts that the health benefits from vitamins and minerals are still uncertain and that vitamins may actually pose health risks for two reasons: They are completely unregulated, so they may be overpriced, ineffective, or improperly labeled; and consumers, hoping to exponentially increase vitamins' beneficial effects, may take megadoses of vitamins that may be toxic at high levels. Kava contends that a much safer alternative is to increase the amount of fruits and vegetables consumed.

As you read, consider the following questions:

1. What toxic effects of vitamins does Kava cite in the viewpoint?
2. Why does the author say that vitamins "provide a false sense of security"?
3. What events led to the establishment of dietary standards, according to Kava?

Excerpted from Ruth Kava, *Vitamins and Minerals: Does the Evidence Justify the Supplements?* (New York: American Council on Science and Health, 1995). Reprinted with permission.

Those who do not support the widespread use of dietary supplements for either insurance or prevention are concerned about two aspects of the use of such products: safety and effectiveness. If a pharmaceutical product is to be sold in this country, the company that wishes to sell it must show that the product is both safe and effective for its intended purpose at the intended level of intake. "Safe" does not mean completely safe for everyone under all possible circumstances, however. Drugs have negative side effects that must be disclosed so that physicians can evaluate whether a particular drug is appropriate for a given patient. Much research and testing is performed to define and establish such guidelines.

No such testing is required of vitamins and minerals, even though they are frequently used in pharmacological doses (doses much larger than could be obtained from foods). Thus, these chemicals (and vitamins and minerals *are* chemicals) may be sold without prior certification that they are either safe or effective for the purposes for which people buy them, and without scientifically established dosage levels for particular purposes. From a legal standpoint, dietary supplements are considered foods, not drugs. Manufacturers thus do not have to prove either safety or efficacy; and according to legislation passed in 1994, if any safety issue arises, it will be up to the Food and Drug Administration (FDA) to prove that a problem exists.

The Dangers of Inaccurate Labeling

There is some cause for concern about the content of some preparations. A 1994 review of the prices and contents of various vitamin and mineral supplements revealed that some were labeled inaccurately. In addition, there was a sixfold range in price for what were essentially the same items. Thus, a consumer can buy a product that is inaccurately labeled, overpriced and possibly ineffective for its intended purpose.

Nutritionists concerned about safety worry about the possibility of negative effects from massive doses of some nutrients; this concern primarily involves the use of supplements of individual nutrients.

The idea that "if a little is good, a lot is better" does not apply to a number of vitamins and minerals, just as it does not apply to over-the-counter medications such as aspirin, to prescription drugs—or even to table salt. But because people view vitamins and minerals as foods and as relatively "natural" products, people tend to be less wary about the possible ill effects of overdoses.

High doses of several nutrients are known to have toxic effects. For example, prolonged high doses of vitamin A (retinol), when taken by pregnant women, lead to liver damage and birth defects. Despite the fact that the water-soluble vitamins—among

Estimated Safe and Toxic Levels of Vitamins and Minerals

Nutrient	Highest Recommended Adult Intake	Estimated Daily Adult Oral Minimum Toxic Dose
Vitamin A (retinol)	5,000 IU (1,000 RE)	25,000 to 50,000 IU
Vitamin D	400 IU (10 mg)	50,000 IU
Vitamin E	30 IU (10 mg α-TE)	1,200 IU
Vitamin C	60 mg	1,000 to 5,000 mg
Thiamin (B_1)	1.5 mg	300 mg
Riboflavin (B_2)	1.8 mg	1,000 mg
Niacin (nicotinamide)	20 mg	1,000 mg
Pyridoxine (B_6)	2.0 mg	2,000 mg
Folacin	0.2 mg	400 mg
Biotin	0.1 mg	50 mg
Pantothenic acid	7 mg	1,000 mg
Calcium	1,200 mg	12,000 mg
Phosphorus	1,200 mg	12,000 mg
Magnesium	400 mg	6,000 mg
Iron	15 mg	100 mg
Zinc	15 mg	500 mg
Copper	3 mg	100 mg
Fluoride	4 mg	4 to 20 mg
Iodine	0.15 mg	2 mg
Selenium	0.07 mg	1 mg

Source: American Council on Science and Health, *Vitamins and Minerals: Does the Evidence Justify Supplements?* 1995.

them vitamin C, vitamin B_6 and niacin—are eliminated from the body relatively quickly, megadoses of such nutrients are not necessarily innocuous. Excess vitamin B_6—used until recently to treat premenstrual syndrome—can impair nervous system function. Megadoses of vitamin C can cause diarrhea and changes in the way the body handles glucose—which could be important to diabetics. Large doses of niacin can also change the way the body handles glucose and can cause liver irritation and unpleasant skin flushing.

There can be negative interactions between nutrients, too, especially when some are taken in very large amounts. Excess zinc intake interferes with the body's use of copper, another essential mineral. Large doses of calcium can diminish the absorption of dietary iron.

Because antioxidant vitamins are currently in vogue, it is important to consider possible problems from large doses of these vitamins. Some recent data suggest that excess intake of antioxidants can be problematic, but there have not yet been any long-term studies of tolerance or toxicity. In fact, an antioxidant substance may not always act as an antioxidant. Under some conditions, it may even act in the opposite way, producing more oxidations instead of suppressing them.

For example, in the presence of excess iron, vitamin C, rather than acting as an antioxidant, becomes just such a pro-oxidant. This could be a problem for people with high levels of LDL ("bad") cholesterol, as oxidation of LDL raises the probability that this cholesterol will form deposits in the arteries. In such cases, high levels of vitamin C taken in part to help protect against heart attack may actually increase the risk. Approximately 10 percent of Americans have an inherited genetic disorder that predisposes them to higher than usual levels of body iron. For these individuals, especially if they also have high levels of LDL cholesterol, megadose vitamin C supplementation could be counterproductive and possibly injurious.

Another argument against the use of dietary supplements is that they provide a false sense of security. Someone who relies too completely on supplements may ignore symptoms of illness or treat them with supplements rather than obtaining medical care. This could allow a disease to progress too far to be treated effectively. Also, a person who takes vitamins and/or minerals may think he or she has fulfilled all dietary requirements and may ignore other important dietary advice. Someone eating a "meat-and-potatoes" diet, for example—a diet containing high levels of saturated fatty acids, few fruits and vegetables and few or no dairy products—may rely on supplements to supply "good nutrition."

Vitamins Are Complex Chemicals

Relying on supplements in this way assumes that our knowledge of important dietary constituents is complete, and that most important nutrients can be obtained from supplements—which is not necessarily true. Foods are extraordinarily complex combinations of hundreds of different chemical compounds, many of which have not yet been investigated for their health effects. Reliance on supplements may lead consumers to miss out on some very important nutrients, as well as nonnutrient components (like fiber) that contribute to health.

There are over 600 different carotenoids, for example. Some of these, like lycopene (from tomatoes) and lutein and zeaxanthin (from spinach), may be better antioxidants than beta-carotene. Other chemicals—like sulforaphane, found in broccoli—activate liver enzymes that inactivate some carcinogenic substances. Because the research on these compounds is still in its early stages, there is little evidence on effective dosage or possible toxicity problems. Indeed, the strongest epidemiological evidence supporting the possible beneficial effects of antioxidants for cancer prevention comes from studies involving fruit and vegetable consumption. Of 156 recent epidemiological studies, 128 found a decreased risk of certain cancers in persons with the highest consumption of fruits and vegetables.

It is true that fruits and vegetables are good sources of antioxidant nutrients. And it is important to remember that beta-carotene, vitamin C and vitamin E are only three among many such compounds—and not necessarily the most effective ones. Also, the efficacy of these nutrients may be increased when they are consumed in combination with other compounds normally found together with them in foods.

Are supplements effective? A recent epidemiological study analyzed dietary and supplementation data from nearly 11,000 people and examined death rates occurring 12 to 16 years after the initial survey. There was no difference in mortality rate, either from all causes or from cancer, between those who reported taking supplements on a regular basis and those who did not.

Although these data argue against the hypothesis that increased vitamin and mineral intake will prolong life, they don't speak directly to the issues raised above about the prevention of chronic diseases. The jury is still out on that question. . . .

Dietary Guides

There is not yet substantial agreement among nutrition experts about the use of vitamin and mineral supplements for prevention of chronic diseases. In contrast, there is very strong evidence that a balanced diet high in fruits and vegetables may really help prevent chronic diseases. What is involved in such diets? Where should the consumer look for scientifically valid guidelines? There are two major sources for such information, the Recommended Dietary Allowances (RDAs) and the Food Guide Pyramid.

As young men were mobilized for military service in the early 1940s, many of them were failing their induction physicals because of conditions related to deficient nutritional status. Partly in response to this situation, the National Research Council (NRC) of the National Academy of Sciences was charged with establishing a set of dietary standards to be used by the military (and other organizations) to ensure the adequacy of nutrient intake for various groups of people. In 1943 the Food and Nutrition Board (FNB) of the NRC published the first edition of the *Recommended Dietary Allowances* (RDAs) in the *Journal of the American Dietetics Association.*

Because nutrient needs change with age and physiological

condition, the RDAs are grouped by gender and age. The allowances are not designed to evaluate the adequacy of nutrient intake by individuals, although they are often used for this purpose. The RDAs are "the levels of intake of essential nutrients that, on the basis of scientific knowledge, are judged by the Food and Nutrition Board to be adequate to meet the known nutrient needs of practically all healthy persons." The nutrient levels set by the RDAs are intended to be an average of a person's intake over a period of time. Thus, if intake does not meet RDA levels on one day, that does not mean a deficiency is imminent.

Because the true nutrient requirements of individuals differ and are not known precisely, the RDAs are set at greater than average requirements for each nutrient (but not for energy). For example, for most healthy adults an average intake of 10 to 15 milligrams of vitamin C would be enough to prevent the deficiency disease scurvy. But to allow for individual variability, the RDA for vitamin C is set at 60 milligrams per day—four to six times more than the minimum.

Because the RDAs are set to meet the requirements of people whose needs are high, they actually will exceed the requirements of most people. Also, since the RDAs are set high, it would be an error to assume that an individual's intake is inadequate or that he or she is at risk of deficiency if his or her intake does not meet or exceed the RDAs. It would be accurate to assume that the farther the average intake falls below the RDAs, the greater the risk of deficiency.

In practice, what is sometimes done is to use a particular cutoff below which the probability of deficiency is said to increase—e.g., two-thirds or 70 percent of the RDA for a given nutrient. Clinical or biochemical tests would be necessary to determine deficiency in a particular individual.

Revising the RDAs

From the start, the RDAs have been revised every five to ten years to include the latest scientific data. The first edition (1943) included only five vitamins and two minerals; the latest (the tenth, issued in 1989) covers 11 vitamins and seven minerals. RDAs are set only when there is agreement among the members of the Food and Nutrition Board committee that adequate scientific data exist to support their decisions. If a nutrient is known to be essential for human health but there is not enough information to establish a recommended dietary level, an Estimated Safe and Adequate Daily Dietary Intake level (ESADDI) will be set.

Another reason to revise the RDAs periodically is to include the latest data on the changing needs of the population. The U.S. population in 1995 includes a greater proportion of elderly people, for example, than it did when the RDAs were first published; and as life expectancy increases, this trend is likely to continue. In addition, larger numbers of elderly people are surviving to quite advanced ages: The average life span is now 76 years, but many individuals today survive well into their 90s.

As the elderly population increases in size, we continue to increase our knowledge about the nutritional needs of both the elderly and the very elderly. It is hoped that we soon will be able to make some more specific age-related nutritional recommendations than are found in the most recent edition of the RDAs, which refers to the oldest age groups simply as "51 + ."

The process of updating the RDAs is under way again. It is possible that the next addition, as well as providing the traditional information directed toward insuring dietary adequacy, will reflect the explosion of recent research relating nutritional status to the risk of chronic diseases. . . .

While intriguing and encouraging, the scientific evidence to date does not provide a firm basis for advocating dietary supplementation in normal, healthy adults to prevent chronic diseases such as cancer and heart disease. Some studies support the idea that some nutrients, in particular the antioxidants, may be protective; but there are also some indications that those nutrients may be at best neutral or—at worst—harmful for some people.

Most intriguing is the possibility that there are even more beneficial compounds in foods than those we currently recognize—compounds that may be even more important. What the data do confirm—and very strongly—is the advice to eat more fruits and vegetables. Although this advice may seem simplistic, the fact remains that only 10 percent of the U.S. population consumes the recommended five servings of fruit and vegetables per day.

The case for calcium is somewhat different. There is an increasing body of evidence suggesting that high calcium intake is important to young women—to help them reach peak bone density and to decrease their risk of osteoporosis later in life. Menopausal or postmenopausal women should also be aware that a high calcium intake may be helpful in slowing bone loss due to diminishing hormone levels. This information is particularly important for those women who do not use hormone-replacement therapy.

While it is likely that the best source for additional calcium remains dairy products, for those who are unable or unwilling to increase their consumption, calcium supplementation is recommended.

ACSH recommends that individuals make dietary decisions in a rational and prudent manner—not as emotional responses to fears of possible deficiency or the lack of some elusive and undefined "optimal" nutrition, and not in response to the latest "hot" media release.

Periodical Bibliography

The following articles have been selected to supplement the diverse views presented in this chapter. Addresses are provided for periodicals not indexed in the *Readers' Guide to Periodical Literature*, the *Alternative Press Index*, or the *Social Sciences Index*.

American Dietetic Association	"Position of the American Dietetic Association: Vegetarian Diets," *Journal of the American Dietetic Association*, November 1993. Available from 216 W. Jackson Blvd., Suite 800, Chicago, IL 60606.
Digby Anderson	"Vegemaniacs," *National Review*, November 1, 1993.
Edna Antonian	"Are Vegetarian Diets Healthful?" *Priorities*, vol. 7, no. 3, 1995. Available from ACSH, 1995 Broadway, 2nd Fl., New York, NY 10023-5860.
Arline Brecher	"Can Vitamins Save Your Life?" *New Age Journal*, January/February 1993. Available from 42 Pleasant St., Watertown, MA 02172.
Marian Burros	"In an About-Face, U.S. Says Alcohol Has Health Benefits," *New York Times*, January 3, 1996.
CQ Researcher	"Dietary Supplements: Should Health Products Be Less Tightly Regulated?" vol. 4, no. 25, July 8, 1994. Available from 1414 22nd St. NW, Washington, DC 20037.
Randi Glatzer	"The Big Queasy," *Mademoiselle*, August 1995.
Suzanne Hamlin	"Eating in 1994: The Year Beef Came Back," *New York Times*, December 28, 1994.
Joseph Hooper	"The Case for Meat: Has the Demonization of Meat Gone Too Far?" *Esquire*, January 1996.
Jane H. Ingraham	"The War on Vitamins," *New American*, November 1, 1993. Available from 770 Westhill Blvd., Appleton, WI 54914.
Gina Kolata	"Study Finds Fish-Heavy Diet Offers No Heart Protection," *New York Times*, April 13, 1994.
Kathleen Meister	"The Skinny on Skim Versus 2% Milk," *Priorities*, vol. 7, no. 2, 1995.
Lauren Mukamal	"Going Vegetarian," *Ms.*, July/August 1994.

Molly O'Neill — "A Question of Ethics Confronts Organic Food Industry," *New York Times*, May 17, 1995.

Psychology Today — "The Cholesterol Conundrum," May/June 1995.

Bill Scanlon — "All but Six Deadly Risks Probably Are Not Worth Avoiding, Odds Show," *Washington Times*, April 2, 1995. Available from Reprints, 3600 New York Ave. NE, Washington, DC 20002.

Linda Strega — "Perfume, Chemicals, and Cancer," *Off Our Backs*, June 1995. Available from 2337B 18th St. NW, Washington, DC 20009.

Fabrizis L. Suarez et al. — "A Comparison of Symptoms After the Consumption of Milk or Lactose-Hydrolyzed Milk by People with Self-Reported Severe Lactose Intolerance," *New England Journal of Medicine*, vol. 333, no. 1, July 6, 1995. Available from 10 Shattuck St., Boston, MA 02115-6094.

Sallie Tisdale — "Meat," *Antioch Review*, Summer 1994. Available from Box 148, Yellow Springs, OH 45387.

Ronald G. Victor and Jim Hansen — "Alcohol and Blood Pressure—a Drink a Day . . . ," *New England Journal of Medicine*, vol. 332, no. 26, June 29, 1995.

Thomas Witherell — "Notes from the Vegetarian Underground," *America*, April 23, 1994.

Yoga Journal — "Space Vegans," November/December 1994. Available from 2054 University Ave., Berkeley, CA 94704.

Barry L. Zalph — "A Quaker Approach to Dietary Concerns," *Friends Journal*, October 1995. Available from 1501 Cherry St., Philadelphia, PA 19102-1497.

Are Exercise and Weight-Loss Treatments Beneficial?

Chapter Preface

According to the American Medical Association, 30 percent of adult Americans are overweight. Many public health officials believe that these individuals suffer adverse health effects due to their excess weight. For example, the U.S. Department of Health and Human Services reports that obesity is associated with "an increased risk for diabetes, heart disease, stroke, hypertension, gallstones, and certain types of cancer."

Losing weight, however, has proven to be extremely difficult for large numbers of people. Diets—including the major weight-loss programs offered by Weight Watchers International, Jenny Craig, and Nutri/System—often help people shed pounds. Nevertheless, most of these dieters regain the lost pounds (many gain more than they initially lost), and some fall into a pattern of "yo-yo dieting"—repeatedly losing weight only to gain it back. Researchers have suggested that one reason it is so difficult to lose weight stems from human biology. Each body, they argue, has a "set point"—a natural weight that the body strives to maintain. When a person loses weight, his or her metabolism automatically compensates to bring the weight back up to its predetermined level.

Due in part to the difficulty in achieving benefits from dieting, many health professionals advocate exercise as a means of losing weight. The issue of exercise is not without controversies. For example, some disagree over the relative merits of moderate versus vigorous workouts. Others warn of the dangers of "exercise addiction"—an unhealthy obsession with exercise. However, experts overwhelmingly agree that physical activity is an essential part of any long-term weight-loss effort. "Some believe [exercise] is even more important than restricting calories," Susan C. Phillips writes in the *CQ Researcher*. "And those who lose weight through diets have a much better chance at keeping the weight off if they exercise regularly." Regular exercise is crucial, health officials argue, because it burns calories and speeds up the body's metabolic rate, both of which combat the accumulation of fat tissue.

Researchers are developing new weapons in the war against fat. Some advocate the use of long-term drug therapy for those considered extremely obese. Others predict that the discovery of an "ob gene"—a gene that regulates hunger—could lead to the development of revolutionary new obesity treatments. Dieting, exercise, and other weight-loss methods are discussed in the following chapter.

"Moderate-intensity physical activity provides substantial health benefits."

Exercise Is Physically Beneficial

The Centers for Disease Control and Prevention
and the American College of Sports Medicine

The Centers for Disease Control and Prevention is an agency of the U.S. government that combats communicable diseases and conducts research in occupational safety and health education. The American College of Sports Medicine is an organization that promotes sports medicine and exercise science and that educates specialists in exercise and fitness. In the following viewpoint, a panel of experts assembled by these two organizations recommends that adults engage in thirty minutes of moderate physical activity (the equivalent of walking three to four miles per hour) every day. They contend that such exercise results in numerous health benefits, including a reduced risk for diseases such as coronary heart disease, hypertension, and colon cancer.

As you read, consider the following questions:

1. How many deaths per year in the United States do the authors say are attributable to a lack of regular physical activity?
2. In what two ways are the new exercise recommendations unique, according to the authors?
3. What do the authors consider to be the benefits of improved muscle strength and flexibility?

Excerpted from the Centers for Disease Control and Prevention and the American College of Sports Medicine, "Physical Activity and Public Health," *JAMA*, vol. 273, no. 5, pp. 402–407, February 1, 1995.

Regular physical activity has long been regarded as an important component of a healthy lifestyle. Recently, this impression has been reinforced by new scientific evidence linking regular physical activity to a wide array of physical and mental health benefits. Despite this evidence and the public's apparent acceptance of the importance of physical activity, millions of US adults remain essentially sedentary.

If our sedentary society is to change to one that is more physically active, health organizations and educational institutions must communicate to the public the amounts and types of physical activity that are needed to prevent disease and promote health. These organizations and institutions, providers of health services, communities, and individuals must also implement effective strategies that promote the adoption of physically active lifestyles.

A group of experts was brought together by the Centers for Disease Control and Prevention (CDC) and the American College of Sports Medicine (ACSM) to review the pertinent scientific evidence and to develop a clear, concise "public health message" regarding physical activity. The panel of experts also considered the organizational initiatives that should be implemented to help US adults become more physically active.

The focus of this viewpoint is on physical activity and the health benefits associated with regular, moderate-intensity physical activity. Physical activity has been defined as "any bodily movement produced by skeletal muscles that results in energy expenditure." Moderate physical activity is activity performed at an intensity of 3 to 6 METs (work metabolic rate/resting metabolic rate)—the equivalent of brisk walking at 3 to 4 mph for most healthy adults. Physical activity is closely related to, but distinct from, exercise and physical fitness. Exercise is a subset of physical activity defined as "planned, structured, and repetitive bodily movement done to improve or maintain one or more components of physical fitness." Physical fitness is "a set of attributes that people have or achieve that relates to the ability to perform physical activity.". . .

Physical Activity and Health

Cross-sectional epidemiologic studies and controlled, experimental investigations have demonstrated that physically active adults, as contrasted with their sedentary counterparts, tend to develop and maintain higher levels of physical fitness. Epidemiologic research has demonstrated protective effects of varying strength between physical activity and risk for several chronic diseases, including coronary heart disease (CHD), hypertension, non-insulin-dependent diabetes mellitus, osteoporosis, colon cancer, and anxiety and depression.

Other epidemiologic studies have shown that low levels of habitual physical activity and low levels of physical fitness are associated with markedly increased all-cause mortality rates. A midlife increase in physical activity is associated with a decreased risk of mortality. It has been estimated that as many as 250,000 deaths per year in the United States, approximately 12% of the total, are attributable to a lack of regular physical activity.

The conclusions of these epidemiologic studies are supported by experimental studies showing that exercise training improves CHD risk factors and other health-related factors, including blood lipid profile, resting blood pressure in borderline hypertensives, body composition, glucose tolerance and insulin sensitivity, bone density, immune function, and psychological function. . . .

Epidemiology of Physical Activity

Physical activity recommendations in *Healthy People 2000* [by the U.S. Department of Health and Human Services] are to "[i]ncrease to at least 30 percent the proportion of people aged 6 and older who engage regularly, preferably daily, in light to moderate physical activity for at least 30 minutes per day." However, only about 22% of adults are active at this level recommended for health benefits, 54% are somewhat active but do not meet this objective, and 24% or more are completely sedentary (ie, reporting no leisure-time physical activity during the past month). Participation in regular physical activity gradually increased during the 1960s, 1970s, and early 1980s, but seems to have plateaued in recent years.

Patterns of physical activity vary with demographic characteristics. Men are more likely than women to engage in regular activity, in vigorous exercise, and sports. The total amount of time spent engaging in physical activity declines with age. Adults at retirement age (65 years) show some increased participation in activities of light to moderate intensity, but, overall, physical activity declines continuously as age increases. African Americans and other ethnic minority populations are less active than white Americans, and this disparity is more pronounced for women. People with higher levels of education participate in more leisure-time physical activity than do people with less education. Differences in education and socioeconomic status account for most, if not all, of the differences in leisure-time physical activity associated with race/ethnicity. . . .

Recommendation for Adults

The current low-participation rate may be due in part to the misperception of many people that to reap health benefits they must engage in vigorous, continuous exercise. The scientific evidence clearly demonstrates that regular, moderate-intensity physical activity provides substantial health benefits. After review of physiological, epidemiologic, and clinical evidence, an expert panel formulated the following recommendation:

Every US adult should accumulate 30 minutes or more of moderate-intensity physical activity on most, preferably all, days of the week.

This recommendation emphasizes the benefits of moderate-intensity physical activity and of physical activity that can be accumulated in relatively short bouts. Adults who engage in moderate-intensity physical activity—ie, enough to expend approximately 200 calories per day—can expect many of the health benefits described herein. To expend these calories, about 30 minutes of moderate-intensity physical activity should be accumulated during the course of the day. One way to meet this standard is to walk 2 miles briskly. Table 1 provides examples of moderate-intensity physical activities.

Table 1—Examples of Common Physical Activities for Healthy U.S. Adults

Light	Moderate	Hard/Vigorous
Walking, slowly (strolling) (1-2 mph)	Walking, briskly (3-4 mph)	Walking, briskly uphill or with a load
Cycling, stationary (<50 W)	Cycling for pleasure or transportation (≤10 mph)	Cycling, fast or racing (>10 mph)
Swimming, slow treading	Swimming, moderate effort	Swimming, fast treading or crawl
Conditioning exercise, light stretching	Conditioning exercise, general calisthenics	Conditioning exercise stair ergometer, ski machine
· · ·	Racket sports, table tennis	Racket sports, singles tennis, racketball
Golf, power cart	Golf, pulling cart or carrying clubs	· · ·
Bowling	· · ·	· · ·
Fishing, sitting	Fishing, standing/casting	Fishing in stream
Boating, power	Canoeing, leisurely (2.0-3.9 mph)	Canoeing, rapidly (≥4 mph)
Home care, carpet sweeping	Home care, general cleaning	Moving furniture
Mowing lawn, riding mower	Mowing lawn, power mower	Mowing lawn, hand mower
Home repair, carpentry	Home repair, painting	· · ·

Russell R. Pate et al., *JAMA*, February 1, 1995.

Intermittent activity also confers substantial benefits. Therefore, the recommended 30 minutes of activity can be accumulated in short bouts of activity: walking up the stairs instead of taking the elevator, walking instead of driving short distances, doing calisthenics, or pedaling a stationary cycle while watching television. Gardening, housework, raking leaves, dancing, and playing actively with children can also contribute to the 30-minute-per-day total if performed at an intensity corresponding to brisk walking. Those who perform lower-intensity activities should do them more often, for longer periods of time, or both.

People who prefer more formal exercise may choose to walk or participate in more vigorous activities, such as jogging, swimming, or cycling for 30 minutes daily. Sports and recreational activities, such as tennis or golf (without riding a cart), can also be applied to the daily total.

Because most adults do not currently meet the standard described herein, almost all should strive to increase their participation in physical activity that is of at least moderate intensity. Those who do not engage in regular physical activity should begin by incorporating a few minutes of increased activity into their day, building up gradually to 30 minutes per day of physical activity. Those who are active on an irregular basis should strive to adopt a more consistent activity pattern.

The health benefits gained from increased physical activity depend on the initial activity level. Sedentary individuals are expected to benefit most from increasing their activity to the recommended level. People who are physically active at a level below the standard would also benefit from reaching the recommended level of physical activity. People who already meet the recommendation are also likely to derive some additional health and fitness benefits from becoming more physically active.

Most adults do not need to see their physician before starting a moderate-intensity physical activity program. However, men older than 40 years and women older than 50 years who plan a vigorous program or who have either chronic disease or risk factors for chronic disease should consult their physician to design a safe, effective program.

Previous Recommendations

The recommendation presented in this viewpoint is intended to complement, not supersede, previous exercise recommendations. In the past, exercise recommendations (including those from the ACSM) were based on scientific studies that investigated dose-response improvements in performance capacity after exercise training, especially the effects of endurance exercise training on maximal aerobic power (maximum oxygen consumption). The recommendations usually involved 20 to 60 minutes of moderate- to high-intensity endurance exercise (60% to 90% of maximum heart rate or 50% to 85% of maximal aerobic power) performed three or more times per week.

Although the earlier exercise recommendations were based on documented improvements in fitness, they probably provide most of the disease prevention benefits associated with an increase in physical activity. However, it now appears that the majority of these health benefits can be gained by performing moderate-intensity physical activities outside of formal exercise programs.

Unique Aspects of the New Recommendation

The new recommendation extends the traditional exercise-fitness model to a broader physical activity–health paradigm. The recommendation is distinct in two important ways. First, the health benefits of moderate-intensity physical activity are emphasized. Second, accumulation of physical activity in intermittent, short bouts is considered an appropriate approach to achieving the activity goal. These unique elements of the recommendation are based on mounting evidence indicating that the health benefits of physical activity are linked principally to the total amount of physical activity performed. This evidence suggests that amount of activity is more important than the specific manner in which the activity is performed (ie, mode, intensity, or duration of the activity bouts).

The health benefits of physical activity appear to accrue in approximate proportion to the total amount of activity performed, measured as either caloric expenditure or minutes of physical activity. For example, observational studies have shown a significantly lower death rate from CHD in people who perform an average of 47 minutes vs 15 minutes of activity per day, and in men who expend an estimated 2000 or more calories per week vs those who expend 500 or fewer calories per week. . . .

Although more research is needed to better elucidate the health effects of moderate- vs high-intensity activity and intermittent vs continuous activity, clinicians and public health practitioners must rely on the most reasonable interpretation of existing data to guide their actions. We believe that the most reasonable interpretation of the currently available data is that (1) caloric expenditure and total time of physical activity are associated with reduced cardiovascular disease incidence and mortality; (2) there is a dose-response relationship for this association; (3) regular moderate physical activity provides substantial health benefits; and (4) intermittent bouts of physical activity, as short as 8 to 10 minutes, totaling 30 minutes or more on most days provide beneficial health and fitness effects.

The preceding recommendation addresses the role of endurance exercise in preventing chronic diseases. However, two other components of fitness—flexibility and muscular strength— should not be overlooked. Clinical experience and limited studies suggest that people who maintain or improve their strength and flexibility may be better able to perform daily activities, may be less likely to develop back pain, and may be better able to avoid disability, especially as they advance into older age. Regular physical activity also may contribute to better balance, coordination, and agility, which in turn may help prevent falls in the elderly. . . .

Enhanced Quality of Life

If Americans who lead sedentary lives would adopt a more active lifestyle, there would be enormous benefit to the public's health and to individual well-being. An active lifestyle does not require a regimented, vigorous exercise program. Instead, small changes that increase daily physical activity will enable individuals to reduce their risk of chronic disease and may contribute to enhanced quality of life.

"Exercise acts as nature's form of Prozac."

Exercise Can Be Psychologically Beneficial

Susan Chollar

In the following viewpoint, Susan Chollar cites various studies and anecdotal examples to support her view that exercise can lift depression, ease anxiety, and boost self-esteem. She argues that exercise produces various physiological reactions in the human body that in turn improve the exerciser's mental state. For example, a vigorous workout raises the body temperature, according to Chollar, producing a tranquilizing effect similar to that caused by a hot bath. Exercise can also correct the brain chemical imbalances that cause depression, she asserts. Chollar is an Aptos, California, writer who specializes in science and health issues.

As you read, consider the following questions:

1. What is Joan Gondola's "Aha!" state, according to Chollar?
2. What neurotransmitters does the author say are increased by exercise? How do these changes affect the mood of the exerciser?
3. According to Chollar, what were the results of Marjorie Klein's study on the psychological effects of exercise?

Sarah Cain loves to run. Most days after work she makes her way along the trails that cut through the redwood forest near her home, leaping over roots that snake across the tree-lined path. And when winter's failing light darkens the forest, she pounds the streets of the small towns that edge California's Monterey Bay. Forty-five miles each week, more than 2,000 miles a year. Year in and year out.

The 35-year-old agricultural research technician likes what exercise does for her body. It keeps her fit, muscular and slim. But she *loves* what it does for her mind. "It keeps me from being depressed and calms me down," she says. "I get a warm, glowing feeling after I run. It takes the edge off."

Although many people are lured to exercise for its well-known cardiovascular benefits or because it makes them look good, a growing number are working up a sweat for the psychological benefits. Exercise can't transform an aggressive, type A personality into a calm type B, but scientists now know that even moderate activity—say, a brisk walk at lunchtime—can lift spirits or dispel tension. And therapists are increasingly prescribing exercise to help their patients cope with more long-term psychological ailments such as anxiety and clinical depression.

A study at the University of Western Australia in Perth, for instance, compared college students in an aerobic dance class with a sedentary group. After their workouts, the dancers scored significantly higher on self-esteem tests than the nonexercisers.

Regular physical activity also improves alertness and energy. Corwyn Mosiman, a 40-year-old optometrist in Watsonville, California, works out during his lunch break four times a week for an hour and a half. "If I don't do it, I get tired in the afternoon," he says. "Exercise gives me a burst of energy that gets me through the day."

Another study at Brooklyn College in New York City found that students enrolled in a swimming class reported having more vigor after spending 30 to 60 minutes in the pool. They also had significantly lower levels of depression, tension and anger. And in a 15-week study at Loma Linda (California) University, a group of overweight, formerly sedentary women reported significantly higher energy levels than controls after walking for 45 minutes, five times a week. "They loved it," says exercise scientist and study author David Nieman. "They kept telling us how great they felt—that they wanted to keep going."

Improving Mood

Exercise also improves mood. "The effects are most obvious immediately after a workout and can last for several hours," says psychologist Thomas Plante at Santa Clara (California) University. Even more important, long-term exercisers seem to possess an overall sense of well-being that extends into other areas of their lives. Dr. Nieman found that after six weeks, the walkers in his study were significantly less stressed than the sedentary women.

"Exercise gives me a better outlook," says Tim Landeck, a 34-year-old teacher in Watsonville, California, who turns to kayaking and trail-biking when the pressures of work and taking care of his two small children get him down. "Afterward, I feel more jazzed up about what I'm doing."

The Exercise High

The exercise high has been linked with two specific phenomena. The first one, which can be reached within weeks, is a consistently attainable elevation of mood. This is the feeling that most athletes talk about, if they are aware of an exercise-induced feeling of emotional and mental well-being.

The second, and rarer, exercise high is a virtual "explosion" of good feeling. Not everyone experiences this special feeling, and you should not make it the goal of your exercise program. If it happens, it is a wonderful bonus, and you will certainly recognize it instantly. The first type of high, however, is consistently satisfying, even exhilarating, and will be the emotional spark to keep you exercising.

Lewis G. Maharam, *Maharam's Curve: The Exercise High—How to Get It, How to Keep It*, 1992.

There's even evidence that exercise helps the creative juices flow. In studies at New York City's Baruch College, exercise psychologist Joan Gondola found that college students who ran regularly or took aerobic dance classes scored significantly higher on a standard psychological test of creativity than students who hadn't exercised. Dr. Gondola says that during her own workouts, she frequently slips into an almost trancelike state where feelings and intuition prevail over more structured thoughts. She calls it her "Aha!" state because creative solutions to nagging problems often pop into her head during those times.

Cognitive Skills

Long-term exercise may also help head off the decline in mental skills, including slowed reaction time and loss of short-term memory, that often accompanies aging. Psychologists Alan Hartley and Louise Clarkson-Smith of Scripps College in Claremont, California, studied 300 men and women 55 and over who were either sedentary or active. The exercisers, who had run the equivalent of six miles a day for many years, scored higher on tests of reaction time, working memory and nonverbal reasoning than did their sedentary counterparts. "By becoming active when you're young, and staying active," says Dr. Hartley, "you're guarding against the mental deterioration that can occur with age and inactivity." (There's no evidence, however, that exercise improves mental skills among the young or middle-aged or that it boosts IQ at any point in life.)

The impact of exercise on cognitive skills in the elderly may be due to superior cardiovascular fitness, which assures adequate blood flow and oxygen transport to the brain and may slow the cell death that accompanies normal aging. The alertness and vigor many people report immediately following exercise may also be linked to increased blood flow to the brain. But exercise also triggers the release of several key neurotransmitters, including epinephrine and norepinephrine, that are known to boost alertness.

Alternatively, exercise's calming effects may be due to the rise in body temperature brought on by a vigorous workout. The core temperature of the average jogger, for instance, rises to over 100°, which produces a brief tranquilizing effect not unlike a lazy soak in a hot tub.

Exercise also reduces tension by desensitizing the body to stress. A vigorous workout stimulates the body to pump out the so-called stress hormones, such as cortisol and epinephrine, that prepare your heart, lungs and muscles for "fight or flight." But regular workouts train the body to react less intensely to stress, leaving exercisers better able to cope with anxiety-provoking events.

Nature's Prozac

Another reason to work up a sweat: Exercise acts as nature's form of Prozac, boosting brain levels of norepinephrine, dopamine and serotonin, three neurotransmitters that elevate mood. Studies have shown that depressed people often have abnormally low levels of these chemicals. Most common antidepressants work by correcting this imbalance, and to some extent, exercise also does.

In fact, exercise may be just as effective as more traditional therapies when it comes to treating psychological ills. In a study of 74 depressed men and women at the University of Wisconsin in Madison, psychologist Marjorie Klein compared the effects of two 45-minute running sessions a week with both meditation and group therapy. After 12 weeks, Dr. Klein found that exercise was just as effective in alleviating depression, and that all three approaches reduced anxiety and tension.

What of the proverbial runner's high, the intense pleasure reported by many exercisers during a long, grueling workout?

65

Beta-endorphins (one of a group of opioids that act within the central nervous system to reduce feelings of pain and induce euphoria) have long been credited with these good feelings. When 13 runners at the University of New Mexico in Albuquerque were given an endorphin-blocking drug before a strenuous 28.5-mile mountain race, their performance wasn't affected, but their moods were: Twelve of the 13 runners reported that they didn't get their usual psychological rush during the second half of the race.

Yet some scientists are skeptical of the endorphin high. "It's not exactly what a scientist would consider a tight story," says neuroscientist Huda Akil at the University of Michigan in Ann Arbor. Some studies show that beta-endorphins increase in the bloodstream during strenuous exercise, but whether they also increase within the brain is unclear. For one thing, endorphins are barred from receptors in the brain's pleasure center by the blood-brain barrier, a biochemical surveillance system that protects the blood supply to the brain. "The high many athletes describe," says Emory University neuropharmacologist Michael Owens, "may not be an opiate-induced euphoria but rather a deep sense of relaxation and well-being."

It's also possible that rhythmic exercise such as swimming or cycling may induce a meditative state that brings deep relaxation. Or a session at the gym may simply provide a timeout from unpleasant thoughts and emotions. That may explain why even a slow walk can banish a bad mood. "In some ways, then, exercise may not be much different from a hobby, meditation or prayer," says Santa Clara's Dr. Plante.

Whatever the mechanism, therapists are increasingly tapping into the prescriptive powers of exercise to help troubled patients. "I don't need to worry about the why," says Concord, New Hampshire–based sports psychologist Kate Hays, who became hooked on exercise 14 years ago during a time of personal crisis. "After a run I come home energized and better able to cope," says Dr. Hays, 51, who now runs three to five miles five times a week, and swims half a mile twice a week. "It made me feel wonderful then, and it still does."

Sarah Cain also discovered the therapeutic power of aerobic exercise in her early 20s, when she was suffering from depression. Now whenever she's anxious or blue, Cain laces up her running shoes and hits the trail. "Back then, I didn't have the discipline to make myself exercise when I was depressed," she says. "Now I do. I know better than to just sit there flopping around the house."

"Exercise is not a long-term solution for depression or anxiety states."

Exercise Can Be Psychologically Harmful

Rebecca Prussin, Philip Harvey, and Theresa Foy DiGeronimo

In the following viewpoint, Rebecca Prussin, Philip Harvey, and Theresa Foy DiGeronimo argue that although exercise can be a beneficial form of treatment for depression and anxiety, it can also lead to exercise addiction—a serious form of dependency that adversely affects the sufferer's personal and professional life. Prussin is the director of inpatient services at St. Luke's/Roosevelt Hospital and an assistant professor of clinical psychiatry at Columbia University in New York. Harvey is the director of clinical research and psychology training at Mt. Sinai School of Medicine in New York. DiGeronimo is a writer whose books include *Raising a Healthy Athlete*.

As you read, consider the following questions:

1. In what way does tolerance contribute to the cycle of exercise addiction, as the authors explain it?
2. According to the authors, why is it incorrect to assume that more exercise will translate into a better mood?
3. How does using exercise to treat anxiety and depression reduce the chances of a full recovery, according to the authors?

For many people suffering from transient mild to moderate depression or anxiety, the benefits of exercise are substantial enough to recommend it as the treatment of first choice. . . .

It's important to keep in mind, however, that persistent depression or anxiety is not always best treated with exercise alone. Although exercise may provide temporary relief for mild, moderate, and even severe depressed moods, there are many cases when it fails to make the symptoms and problems go away completely. Even in these cases, exercise may provide a temporary benefit. The problem is that symptoms are partially or temporarily reduced but not eliminated. Therefore, because exercise has the potential to reduce symptoms temporarily without effectively eliminating them it also has the potential to create a dependence without providing a cure. . . .

An Addictive Cycle

Exercise is good therapy for some people with negative mood disorders; for others it is ineffective and even counterproductive. The line between effective self-treatment and addiction is drawn at the point where the depressed or anxious person becomes dependent on exercise while trying to maintain an acceptable degree of mood functioning.

Both dysthymia [chronic depression that is less severe than major depression] and anxiety symptoms affect a person's mood "more often than not." Many people suffering these maladies find that exercise can tip this imbalance and allow them to experience positive feelings (particularly in the self-esteem dimension) more frequently than not. Unfortunately, in many cases the lift generated by exercise is short-lived and the exercise routine must soon be repeated to maintain or regain the mood elevation. Thus, an addictive cycle begins.

Your body develops a tolerance for the amount of exercise that you initially found eased the impact of a mood disorder. Quite naturally, there is a tendency to increase the intensity, duration, and frequency of the exercise program to maintain the same level of benefits. As your body becomes conditioned to expect more intense workouts, the positive effects have the potential to become shorter-lived (sometimes lasting no longer than the time of the actual workout). This is when cravings can develop and you'll find that your exercise routine takes precedence over things that were formerly more important. Once exercise achieves this priority status, your positive moods may become dependent upon a workout.

For a long time, you may feel that the energy and time spent working out is worth all that must be given up for it. It's a trade-off that makes sense as long as the workouts remain less in control of your life than your former misery was. After a while, however, the previously contented exerciser can no longer find the same lift and needs to increase the intensity, duration, or even frequency of the exercise session. Soon the workouts will cause as much distress as the former negative moods and the trade-off will become unacceptable.

Some exercise addicts exercise excessively in the mistaken belief that continuous exercise can prevent the occurrence of future episodes of depression or anxiety. Although there is no evidence that this is possible, it's easy to understand that exercisers might superstitiously cling to their regimens in the belief that they are warding off unpleasant experiences. Certainly if you found that in the past exercise was able to ease the effects of depression or anxiety, you might get caught up in the fear that if you stop exercising you'll risk a return of the problem. And so you'd unknowingly instigate a case of exercise addiction to accommodate this faulty belief.

More Is Not Better

Some excessive exercisers, especially runners, have heard via the grapevine that intense long-distance running relieves negative moods by giving the body and mind a boost through aerobic-based release of endorphins, opiatelike substances found in the brain that can produce the same euphoric and pain-relieving effects as externally administered opiates. Many excessive exercisers believe there is a linear relationship between amount of exercise, release of endorphins, and degree of depression and anxiety relief. The longer you run, some believe, the greater the mood elevation will be. However, this theory does not hold up scientifically.

New studies have found a simpler relationship between exercise and mood improvement. One research team discovered that both running and nonaerobic activities such as weight lifting, equivalent only to a college physical education class, offer an equivalently marked positive mood change. Apparently it is not the kind or degree of exercise that fosters mood improvement but simply the ability of participants to conceptualize themselves as exercisers. In fact, the extent to which participation actually alters the level of a person's self-esteem and mood is not related to the extent of improved aerobic fitness levels. Thus, harder work doesn't necessarily mean a better mood. When people engage in activity that is socially acceptable and positive, they feel good about themselves just because they do it.

The downside of this discovery is that it makes mood-related exercise addiction a more likely possibility in a wider range of exercise modes than was originally thought. As exercisers of all types can find mood alteration in small doses of almost any physical activity, they may arrive at the faulty conclusion that "If a little is good, a lot will be better." And so they double their exercise time seeking double benefits. Because the positive results can be short-lived, the exercisers may return to the specific activity more and more frequently. They find out too late that, as with other addictive substances and activities, more is not better.

Not a Long-Term Solution

The problem with using exercise as a means of mood elevation is that its short-term positive effects cloud its overall long-term ineffectiveness. Yes, exercise can relieve the impact of depression and anxiety in many people and leave them relatively free of these mood disorders, but for many others, the positive effects of exercise kick in rapidly but last for no more than an hour. If the severity of the depression or anxiety is significant enough or persistent enough, the negative feelings will reappear as soon as the exercise session is over, or even begin to intrude into the exercise session itself. Thus, repeated frequent doses of intense exercise will be required to reduce the emotional symptoms adequately.

Exercise Addicts

When the starting gun goes off at any big-city marathon, a motley throng of runners will stream forward: veteran racers, dedicated amateurs, middle-aged first-timers, young guys out on a dare.

Scattered among these will also be an unusually intense group of athletes: men and women who run because of psychological compulsion, emotional fixation, who cannot *not* run.

Some call them "exercise addicts." But that suggests a physical craving, when their behavior is really rooted in the psyche. These are people whose entire lives revolve around their training regimens.

Madeline Drexler, *San Diego Union-Tribune*, November 20, 1994.

What happens to your mood when you don't get your exercise fix? If you have found that your mood problem is relieved by exercise, you may have increased the duration and frequency of your workouts to gain greater psychological benefits. You may have also found that when you are not exercising your moods are still negative and that you have forfeited a great deal in terms of social, occupational, family, and personal interests in your efforts to treat your mood problem. Most likely, you have learned that exercise is not a long-term solution for depression or anxiety states.

Even in the best-case scenario, in which exercise is used successfully to treat negative moods, exercise is not always a complete cure. Research data suggest that exercise has its primary effect on self-esteem or self-image. Thus, exercise may not alleviate the secondary problems, such as insomnia, loss of appetite, or poor concentration. So although some individuals are still suffering to some degree, exercise might keep them from seeking and implementing additional and alternate methods of mood management that, when combined with moderate exercise, have persistently shown positive results. These include medication, psychotherapy, relaxation techniques, and stress-management strategies. By ignoring other avenues of help, some people who are self-treating depression or anxiety with exercise are reducing their chances for a full recovery. This, of course, endangers their capacity for full psychological functioning in the future.

A Miracle Cure

Dan is a thirty-year-old account executive with a large mail-order firm who suffers from an exercise addiction caused by anxiety. A year ago, he sought psychiatric help after his medical internist couldn't find an organic cause for his recurring episodes of muscle aches, general fatigue, dizziness, pounding heart, insomnia, and irritability. He had initially thought that he had a heart condition of some type. But he was eventually diagnosed as having generalized anxiety disorder and began psychotherapy to address his incessant worrying about things that most probably would never happen.

During this time, Dan's wife, too, was eager to help him regain a sense of calm. When she saw him start to show signs of anxiety, she would encourage him to join her in a jog around the lake because she had heard that running was an effective relaxation technique. Initially, Dan was less than enthusiastic about this idea. He had never been much of an athlete; his exercising had been limited to college intramurals and an occasional picnic softball or volleyball game. "I've told you," he'd complain, "that my muscles hurt and that I'm tired and dizzy. You don't understand if you think I should get up and run." But later, Dan's therapist also suggested exercise as a possible source of relief, so Dan gave it a try the next time he found himself falling victim to another round of useless, worrisome thoughts.

After his first few runs around the lake, Dan was delighted to find that for the first time in more than two years he could short-circuit his anxiety attacks with a ten- to twenty-minute run. It was as if someone had handed him a miracle cure. At his next session, Dan explained his new plan of attack to his therapist. "If I run every morning," he reasoned, "I shouldn't have any more problems with anxiety, and hopefully"—he smiled to show he meant no offense—"I won't be seeing you much longer."

The following week, Dan returned to report his progress. "I felt great every day after running before work; now I'm planning to add more distance each day because I figure the longer I run, the more benefit I'll gain. At work I still start to feel lightheaded and tense so I'm thinking about running at lunchtime too. This is great," Dan beamed. "No drugs, no therapy, no problems, *and* I'm getting back into good shape!"

Dependent on Exercise

Eventually, Dan canceled all appointments with his therapist, and the therapist heard nothing more from Dan until seven months later when he called the office after suffering an intense anxiety attack. As the story unfolded, Dan explained that until two weeks earlier he had been running each morning and evening. He used this exercise routine to ward off anxiety and found it so vital to his mental health that he put aside other priorities and obligations he would otherwise have fulfilled in those time periods he now rigidly devoted to exercise.

Dan had developed a tolerance for his original quick runs, so he needed to add additional miles to gain the same physical and mental benefits. He also found himself craving his runs and canceling family and business appointments to satisfy the urge and to calm his fears. Then he fell down a flight of stairs while moving some boxes into the attic. Dan hurt his left knee and couldn't run for at least a month.

Because Dan's ability to function normally had become dependent on exercise he was now experiencing a return of his anxiety symptoms. His original problem with anxiety gradually returned along with an abrupt onset of difficulties associated with the compounding addiction problems. "I feel so sluggish," he confessed. "I have no appetite; I can't sleep; my head hurts, and I feel useless and angry. What's happening? I feel worse now than I did when I first came to you!" Dan returned to his therapist for an answer to his question and also because he had lost the support of his family and friends who had become tired of coming in second to exercise and didn't want to hear his complaining now that he had to spend more time at home. Dan had temporarily lost the external mechanism that enabled him to feel good about himself. Without exercise, Dan had lost his "cure" for anxiety, his self-esteem, and his ability to function in the manner necessary to his work and personal life.

In moderate amounts, exercise could have helped Dan deal with his problems and given him enough time and objectivity to seek additional forms of help. Unfortunately, Dan, like many others who use exercise to self-treat anxiety or depression, fell hard for the idea that more is better. Now Dan and his therapist had to find a way to help him use alternate types of exercise that could be practiced with a bad knee; Dan had to ease himself into a program that would reduce the frequency of exercise and maintain his self-esteem. Dan and his therapist had to return to the original problem of his mood disorder and start again to look for a way to help him function calmly and happily.

"Many medical experts believe they have found a safe and effective weapon against obesity in a selection of drugs."

Drug Treatments for Weight Loss Are Beneficial

David Stipp

Every year, many people fail in their attempts to lose weight by means of diets and exercise. In the following viewpoint, David Stipp, a senior writer for *Fortune* magazine, argues that the obesity with which these people are burdened is a disease that can be treated with long-term drug therapy. He writes that one specific combination of drugs, fenfluramine and phentermine (fen-phen), has produced dramatic results by suppressing appetite and speeding the burning of calories. Stipp argues that other similarly effective drugs, currently being developed and/or used in the United States and abroad, should be approved for domestic use.

As you read, consider the following questions:

1. What proportion of the U.S. population is overweight, according to Stipp?
2. According to the author, what is the ob gene? What theory does he say has received increased credibility due to the discovery of the ob gene?
3. What side effects does Stipp say are associated with fen-phen?

Americans are so aware of their weight that even brownies on the grocery shelves cry "fat free" to catch the attention of the righteous, and closets across the land are stocked with jogging shoes. So the U.S. must be shedding ugly pounds by the millions, right? Unfortunately, no. The surprising and depressing reality is that the nation's collective girth has ballooned over the past decade and a half. When Americans stepped on the scale in 1980, a quarter were overweight. Now the rolls of the fat have swollen to one-third of the population.

But there's also some soothing news for the nation's bulging paunch. Many medical experts believe they have found a safe and effective weapon against obesity in a selection of drugs. One treatment has become so popular that physicians have quadrupled the number of prescriptions they write for it. In the near future, the Food and Drug Administration—so cautious that it hasn't approved a new diet drug in 23 years—may allow several new ones to go on the market. And just over the horizon, maybe, is an innovative generation of treatments based on accumulating knowledge about the genetic roots of obesity.

The potential for the pharmaceutical industry is enormous. Consider: About 58 million adults carry enough extra weight to put them at some health risk. Not all of them will want—or qualify for—drug treatment, but enough will so that Wall Street is smelling the bacon. When scientists working on a gene owned by Amgen announced in July 1995 a protein that made mice lose weight, the market capitalization of the dynamic biotech company jumped by over $900 million, to $11.2 billion.

Obesity as a Disease

What's driving this new enthusiasm for drugs is a growing conviction among many doctors that obesity is a disease. Backing them up is increasing evidence that genetic factors account for a sizable part of the national obesity crisis. Many people seem to be genetically misprogrammed for an era of abundance; they lack the internal signals by which body and mind tell each other that the danger of starvation is long past—so drop the forks.

Because obesity is an illness, these authorities maintain, it makes sense to treat the condition not solely with diet and exercise but in many cases with drugs as well. What they have in mind is not just a quick series of pills to trim some pounds off. They want to prescribe long-term, perhaps lifetime, drug therapies, just as they might for hypertension. Obesity's victims, these doctors hope, will not only be able to take pounds off but will also keep them off forever.

What does one have to weigh to qualify as obese? That's difficult to say. Doctors have no precise definition of obesity. But if you think the paunch you've acquired or the hips you've padded

75

since college are harmless, pay attention. Many medical experts maintain that if you have swollen to 20% above your ideal weight, you are living in a dangerous zone. "If we could get the entire population within 20% of ideal weight, we'd probably have 80% fewer cases of diabetes, which is a leading cause of kidney failure and heart disease," says Dr. Louis Aronne, director of the weight-loss center at prestigious New York Hospital–Cornell Medical Center. As many as 300,000 early deaths might be prevented annually—far more than the number dying each year from AIDS, drug abuse, and other high-profile killers—and the nation's health bill might drop by $70 billion.

Fen-Phen

The overweight men and women flocking to places like Biochemical Medical Care certainly feel pill-assisted slimming is just what the doctor should have ordered years ago. Housed in a nondescript gray-brick building in Monsey, New York, a leafy hamlet 25 miles from New York City, Biochemical is one of a number of recently opened weight-loss clinics that specialize in treating obesity with "fen-phen," a combination of the drugs fenfluramine and phentermine. Fenfluramine boosts serotonin, the same brain chemical that Prozac enhances to elevate mood, while phentermine mimics other substances in the brain. Together the medicines suppress appetite and speed the burning of calories. Fen-phen has rapidly emerged over the past three years as the heavy artillery in the battle of the bulge. Since Biochemical opened in March 1995, some 700 people have signed on to its program [as of December 1995], says cofounder Dr. Ronald DiScenza. Most return every few weeks for examinations and additional supplies of the prescription drugs.

One evening Howard Hutson, 39, briskly strode into the clinic 69 pounds lighter than on his first visit in July 1995, and sat down to wait for an exam with a dozen other determined-looking patients. He's hoping to subtract another 150 pounds from the 381 still straining his 6-foot 3-inch frame—a reasonable goal, he believes, now that fen-phen has checked his food cravings. Says he: "My main problem was always snacking and watching TV. Now I've started to push food away before finishing it."

Not everyone in the medical community is applauding the new therapies. Conservatives are aghast, worried that the new drugs are, in fact, more snake oil from the shamans of lite. Their concerns are understandable. A few decades ago amphetamines—"uppers" or "speed" as they're known in street slang—were widely prescribed to control weight. Patients got prettier figures but paid for them with raw nerves, higher pulse rates, and sleepless nights, symptoms that may have offset the medical benefits of fewer pounds. Conservatives also point out that risky as amphetamines were, they were generally prescribed only for temporary use. Advocates of new drug treatments leave open the possibility that the medicines will be prescribed for a lifetime.

Many conservative doctors, moreover, remain reluctant to diagnose obesity as a disease. In a 1987 survey of 318 physicians, two-thirds said their obese patients lacked self-control, and 39% described them as "lazy." That kind of analysis leads to a bracing, spartan argument that has considerable appeal to the puritan in all of us: Obesity results from a lack of discipline and can be corrected with diet and exercise.

Drug Therapy at Work

How fat was Marcus Williams? At his 500-pound peak, Williams had to sit at the table sideways in order to reach his plate. Blocked by his belly, he couldn't get a good grip on the steering wheel. And the logistical problems were nothing compared with obesity's impact on his health. He developed an irregular heartbeat, high blood pressure, knee problems, varicose veins and diabetes. All this by age 32. . . .

On March 18, 1995, Williams and his wife, Penny, 39, entered the newest frontier of obesity management: treating it not as a character flaw but as a physiological disorder that requires medication. The Williamses expect their drug therapy to last as long as they do. Marcus, who had lost some weight on his own, started the program at 331 pounds; Penny, at 218 pounds. By May, they had dropped 31 and 20 pounds, respectively. Williams says he is satisfied with less food than before.

Rita Rubin, *U.S. News & World Report*, May 15, 1995.

Trouble is, that regimen hasn't worked, not yet at least. As a nation, like T.S. Eliot's J. Alfred Prufrock, we have wept and fasted, wept and prayed—collectively shedding millions of pounds. Indeed, at any one time about a third of us are dieting. We spend about $33 billion a year on super-low-calorie drinks, exercycles, diet books, fitness clubs, and such, but to no avail. A pound lost is generally regained in five years.

The conservative case seems to be losing ground in the medical establishment, not just because it has failed in practice but because it is wobbling a bit in theory as well. In 1994 a research group at Rockefeller University discovered in experiments on mice what has come to be called the obesity, or ob, gene. That revelation led to the identification of a hormone, dubbed leptin, that signals the brain how much fat is stored in the body. When injected into the rodents, the hormone lessened appetite and increased the burning of calories. Studies on ob have greatly boosted the credibility of the decades-old idea that the body has a fat thermostat whose level is largely determined by genes— and have also accelerated the race to develop drugs based on such genetic malfunctions.

The ob discovery was followed by a landmark report in the spring of 1995 from the Institute of Medicine, part of the National Academy of Sciences. An institute panel declared obesity to be a chronic disease, noting among other things that genes may account for a third of the variation in weight across the population. The report made a strong case for stronger remedies to address America's epidemic of obesity, including drug therapy. In a section urging the FDA to lower hurdles for approval of new drugs, the panel wrote that the U.S. has lagged "far behind other countries in the approval and use of anti-obesity drugs."

Shifting the Paradigm

For now, the only diet drug commonly prescribed in the U.S. is the fen-phen combination that Howard Hutson and his comrades are taking. Doctors once prescribed it mainly for brief use by the "morbidly" obese (those who have a disease associated with their weight problem) to help shed pounds when all else failed. But in 1992 a widely publicized study at the University of Rochester showed that patients who took the drugs during a diet and exercise program dropped an average of 21 extra pounds, compared with those on a placebo, and kept most of the weight off for over three years while continuing on fen-phen. Soon after, demand for the drugs took off like the calorie count on Thanksgiving.

Says New York's Dr. Aronne: "I remember thinking, 'Medication? Never!' But when you see some of these patients and the results with drugs, it shifts the paradigm." Aronne and his colleagues still recommend diet and exercise, but drugs have definitely become part of the model recovery program. Capitalizing on the shift in medical thinking, two hefty players in the slimming business—Physicians Weight Loss Centers and Nutri/System—recently began offering fen-phen as part of weight-loss programs at physician-staffed centers. Revenues at Nutri/System's first four NutriRx centers doubled in a little over a month after they introduced fen-phen in September 1995. In November the chain opened five more fen-phen centers. (Both companies are privately owned and don't disclose revenues or earnings. But *Diet Business Bulletin*, an industry newsletter, estimates that Nutri/System had revenues of perhaps as much as $250 million in 1994, and Physicians Weight Loss about one-tenth that.)

Prescriptions are being written so fast that doctors and pharmacies in some places have recently had trouble getting enough fenfluramine, which is sold under the name Pondimin by American Home Products' Wyeth-Ayerst Laboratories division. Prescriptions of fenfluramine in 1995 were expected to be four times what they were in 1994, according to IMS America, which tracks pharmaceutical sales.

The excitement about fen-phen—and the anticipation of even better drugs—is not hard to explain. To the obese, their condition is devastating. They live in a world in which even the shapely think of themselves as too fat. Diligent researchers in Chicago and Toronto reported a significant slimming trend after 1959 among Miss America contestants and *Playboy* centerfolds. So imagine the despair of those who are double the size of what federal health officials call perfection. In a 1991 report on formerly obese people who had lost at least 100 pounds each, some 90% said they would rather be blind or have a leg amputated than gain back their excess pounds.

A Miracle Drug

Deborah Bell, 48, of Gahanna, Ohio, considers fen-phen a miracle drug. For years she fought the good fight against fat—and lost. Anything but lazy, she would diet with steely resolve and shed 20 pounds, then gain back 30, lose 30 and gain 40, her self-esteem and willpower wilting as her weight inexorably rose to 220 pounds. "I was always the fat girl who tried to dress nice," she says. But by her mid-40s, the normally upbeat surgical nurse despaired. "As hard as you try, you find yourself standing in the kitchen eating."

In 1995 Bell dropped 80 pounds and is holding steady at 140. Now she has to curb her gregarious streak: "When I was heavy, I could semiflirt with the men I worked with, and I was safe. Now I have to watch out." The credit for this wonderful problem, she says, goes mostly to fen-phen, which she's taken daily since February 1995. Bell is participating in a five-year study at a Columbus weight-loss clinic on the use of the drugs to help prevent weight rebound after dieting. For her, taking fen-phen feels "like someone lifts this food demon out of your body. I got so excited at first when my food urges were controlled that I didn't eat enough and got scolded by my dietitian for skipping lunch."

For a couple of reasons, however, fen-phen is not the ideal and ultimate diet drug combination. First, there is some debate over safety. Most fen-phen researchers say the drugs pose minor health risks compared with amphetamines. For most patients the short-term side effects are offsetting—phentermine heightens alertness while persuading the body to burn more calories, and fenfluramine, thought to cut cravings for starches and sweets, can induce drowsiness. But some users experience a racing heartbeat and, although rarely, high blood pressure.

Some states ban fen-phen outright, and others limit the length of time a patient can take it. Says James R. Winn, executive vice president of the Federation of State Medical Boards: "The long-term use of diet drugs is extremely controversial. There's a strong likelihood weight clinics will abuse these drugs." And even though its effects are milder than those of amphetamines, the feeling of higher energy that fen-phen stirs can be habit-forming. Also, some patients who quit these drugs abruptly lapse into depression. Warns William Schmidt, an official of Ohio's medical board: "I have to tell you flat out that phenter-mine is abused. We've had a doctor lose his license because he became addicted to phentermine, and others have been disci-plined for overprescribing it." Used alone, phen has enough kick to appeal to recreational drug users, who call it "bumblebee."

Some researchers assert that fenfluramine may damage nerve endings in the brain. There also are scattered reports of short-term memory loss among patients taking the drugs. A spokes-woman for Wyeth-Ayerst counters that fenfluramine has been used by 50 million people worldwide for a period of 30 years, yet no pattern suggestive of nerve damage has appeared. Fen-phen received some helpful support in September 1995 when an FDA advisory panel recommended that fenfluramine be dropped from the federal list of controlled substances.

Even so, fen-phen is not entirely effective. The Rochester study triggering the fen-phen stampede showed that over sev-eral years, subjects taking the drugs tended to regain some of the weight they had lost—albeit at a slower rate than those who didn't take them. Some people get no benefit from them. Says Judith Stern, a nutrition professor at the University of California at Davis: "We're at the same point with obesity drugs that we were with hypertension drugs in 1958, which weren't nearly as good as the ones on the market today."

New Drugs

The pace of progress may pick up soon. The FDA is consider-ing an application by American Home Products to market the diet drug dexfenfluramine, which works on the brain in much the same way as fenfluramine but apparently more effectively and with fewer side effects. As with fen-phen, some researchers worry about animal studies that show heavy doses can cause nerve damage, a concern that in September 1995 erupted into a fiery argument before an FDA advisory panel. But dex has been used in Europe and elsewhere for ten years by about ten million people who have suffered no obvious harm. So there's a reason-able chance the FDA will allow it to go on the market in the U.S. Approval would likely give a big boost to Interneuron Pharmaceuticals, the small Lexington, Massachusetts, biotech company that has developed the drug and licensed it to AHP. Interneuron, seven years old and publicly traded, had revenues of a mere $606,000 in 1995.

People who regard obesity as a disease can't wait to get their hands on these new—but still unapproved—drugs. In fact, some of them aren't waiting. When Eileen Marshall, a self-employed health care consultant in New York City, returned from a vacation in France in the summer of 1995, she carried a year's supply of dex purchased at a Paris pharmacy. After her weight rose above 270 pounds, Marshall, 50, seemed a perfect candidate for fen-phen, because she lost pounds on diets but never kept them off, putting her on a collision course with the diabetes that runs in her family. But for her, fenfluramine caused intolerable diarrhea. After trimming 35 pounds on a weight-loss program in 1994, she decided to try dex.

Says Marshall, a composed, articulate woman who works from a home office on Manhattan's East Side: "If the FDA hasn't approved this drug when I run out of it, I'll have to go back to France and get some more. This is the first time I've been able to keep weight off without going crazy. I don't understand the thinking that it's okay to treat the effects of obesity with drugs but not the obesity itself." Finally, it seems, the medical community is catching up with her reasoning.

"There is no evidence that the deleterious effects of lifelong diet drugs justify the slight, if permanent, weight loss."

Weight-Loss Treatments Are Harmful and Unnecessary

Sally E. Smith

Sally E. Smith is the executive director of the National Association to Advance Fat Acceptance, a Sacramento, California, organization that works to reduce discrimination against obese people. In the following viewpoint, Smith argues that the health risks of obesity have been exaggerated and that attempts at weight loss, including diets and drug treatments, are usually unsuccessful and are often medically dangerous. Rather than attempting to make obese people thin, she asserts, researchers should focus on finding ways to maintain and improve their health.

As you read, consider the following questions:

1. What percentage of dieters does Smith say regain weight?
2. According to the author, what standards has the Federal Trade Commission established to regulate maintenance claims by diet programs?
3. As Smith describes it, how does the diet industry prey on the low self-esteem of overweight people?

Sally E. Smith, "The Great Diet Deception," *USA Today* magazine, January 1995. Copyright 1995 by the Society for the Advancement of Education. Reprinted with permission.

While weight loss potions and gizmos have been in existence since the 1800s, the modern day weight loss business has ballooned into a multi-billion-dollar industry. It is impacting individuals' health negatively, promoting social stigma and discrimination against fat people, and generating unconscionable conflicts of interest among public health policymakers. For years, the commercial weight loss industry was largely unregulated. Only recently, due to Congressional pressure, have the Federal Trade Commission (FTC) and the Food and Drug Administration (FDA) begun to enforce existing regulations. These are narrow in scope, however, and it seems clear that more drastic measures must be taken to protect public health.

In his book, *Never Satisfied: A Cultural History of Diets, Fantasies, and Fat,* Hillel Schwartz traces the early days of the weight loss industry, a succession of 19th-century remedies for fatness ranging from mechanical horses to galvanic belts to specific eating strategies and the myriad of diet foods, drugs, reducing products, and publications available in the 1980s. He writes that the handful of published pieces on weight loss in the late 18th century is "a far cry from the 6,397 technical works on obesity published between 1964 and 1979; a far cry from the 300 diet books in print in the United States in 1984; a far cry from the average of 1.25 dieting articles per issue in the *Ladies Home Journal, Good Housekeeping,* and *Harper's Bazaar* between 1980 and 1984, or the 66 articles on dieting that appeared in 22 contemporary magazines in January of 1980."

Indeed, by 1990, the revenues of the commercial weight loss industry totaled more than $30,000,000,000. According to Marketdata Enterprises, $8,000,000,000 was spent on diet centers and programs; group and individual weight loss; diet camps; prepackaged foods; over-the-counter and prescription drugs; weight loss books and magazines; and physicians, nurses, nutritionists, and other professionals specializing in weight loss. Commercial and residential exercise clubs with weight loss programs brought in an additional $8,000,000,000, and revenues from sugar-free, fat-free, and reduced-calorie food products, imitation fats, and sugar substitutes amounted to more than $14,000,000,000.

Economic Interests

It is no coincidence that the commercial weight loss industry has become a fixture in U.S. society and that its messages have colored the way most Americans view themselves and others. In his book, *Lifespan,* Thomas Moore makes the connection between the evolution of obesity as a disease needing treatment and the economic interests of major players in the field. As evidence, he points to the 1985 National Institutes of Health (NIH) consensus conference, which not only proclaimed obesity a "killer disease," but arbitrarily redefined it in such a way as to affect millions more Americans. This redefinition and the call to arms for treatment translated into billions of additional dollars of research money, commercial weight loss industry profits, and physicians' revenues.

Moore revealed that leading obesity researchers had an enormous economic stake in seeing expanded forms of obesity treatment applied to more Americans. Theodore Van Itallie, chairman of the NIH consensus conference planning committee and a researcher at Columbia University, was a paid consultant to United Weight Control. George Blackburn and Thomas Wadden, considered to be leading authorities in obesity research, were on the payroll of Sandoz, the makers of Optifast, a liquid diet product.

An Obsession with Thinness

American society has an obsession with thinness. With this obsession come open intolerance and oppression against fat individuals. We've all heard the stereotypes. Fat and ugly. Fat and lazy. Fat slobs. Fat people smell. Fat people are stupid. Ann Landers called fat people unsightly. Madonna has been quoted as saying that she would rather be dead than be fat.

A fat person is bombarded with negative feedback from every angle. Family members say, "You have such a pretty face, but . . ." People in grocery stories inspect the items in your basket. You don't even have to leave your house to hear it, just turn on the TV, read a magazine, listen to the radio. You'll hear it. And it is ugly. For a fat person living through this hell, the subliminal message is: "If you would be thin, you would be accepted."

Suzanne Szames, *San Diego Union-Tribune*, April 27, 1994.

This conflict of interest continues, with commercial weight loss and pharmaceutical firms underwriting a significant number of obesity studies. Obesity researchers' professional conferences routinely are funded by commercial interests. The 1991 conference of the North American Association for the Study of Obesity was underwritten by no less than 18 diet companies, pharmaceutical firms, and manufacturers of diet foods, including Sandoz, Weight Watchers, Eli Lilly, Jenny Craig, Nutri/Systems, Upjohn, and Hoffman-LaRoche. Welcoming packets at such conferences often include products from these companies, and, more often than not, sponsors' pre-packaged diet foods are served during conference breaks. Moore writes, "It turns out that most [medical obesity experts] are either consultants to the major companies, conducting research for these companies, presenting their results at conferences sponsored by these companies, or sometimes all three."

Diets Don't Work

While weight loss diets and products long have been promoted as a permanent cure for obesity, they rarely produce long-lasting results. According to medical research, fewer than five percent of all dieters succeed in losing a significant amount of weight and maintaining that loss over a five-year period. Ninety percent of all dieters regain some or all of the weight originally lost, and at least one-third gain more. An increasing amount of research has substantiated these failure rates and acknowledged genetic and physiological factors in the determination of body size.

Diet promoters emphasize the supposed health benefits and minimize risks related to dieting. People of all sizes are being misled about the extent and severity of the health risks associated with being fat and are told that being thin is the only way to good health and that dieting makes people thin. Many medical conditions traditionally attributed to obesity—such as high blood pressure, elevated cholesterol, and heart and gallbladder problems—often can be caused by the dieting process itself. Recent studies indicate that repeated "yo-yo" dieting may reduce one's lifespan.

These findings, which validate the experiences of fat people who have spent years resisting their body's natural predisposition and have struggled harder to lose weight, have had a dramatic impact on the obesity research community. If, indeed, diets don't work, what options are available to researchers who have depended on diet industry funding and who have dedicated their lives to answering the question, "How can we make fat people thin?"

The Pharmaceutical Bandwagon

A natural paradigm shift for obesity researchers would be to discard attempts to make fat people thin and focus on finding ways to maintain and improve their health. Such a shift has not occurred, though. Instead, scientists are hearkening back to the 1960s and 1970s, when diet pills were the rage. Researchers are positioning obesity next to hypertension, as a chronic disease requiring lifelong treatment, even though there is no evidence that obesity significantly decreases longevity. Further, there is no evidence that the deleterious effects of lifelong diet drugs justify the slight, if permanent, weight loss. Nevertheless, jumping onto the pharmaceutical bandwagon by studying and prescribing phentermine and fenfluramine, researchers once again are assured of deep pockets for further studies and conference sponsorships.

In listening to diet and weight loss promoters hawking their programs and products, one would think that permanent thinness is just a phone call or purchase away. If consumers believe the commercial weight loss industry, as most dieters do, a person need only to take a pill, wear a body suit, buy a pre-packaged food plan, or go to weekly meetings to look like a fashion model. As evidence of the ease of the process, weight loss hucksters make wide-ranging claims about the safety, effectiveness, and permanence of their programs and products.

The Government's Role

Historically, the government looked the other way, rarely enforcing what few regulations could be applied to a business that had no industry standards or laws governing its operations. It wasn't until 1990, when Rep. Ron Wyden (D.-Ore.) convened hearings on the diet industry through the Subcommittee on Regulation, Business Opportunities, and Energy, that the spotlight began to shine on the omnipresent deception and fraud and the government's lack of action.

During the Congressional hearings, the FDA, FTC, Federal Communications Commission, and the Attorney General were taken to task for their laxity in enforcing existing regulations. Once the heat was turned up, the FDA investigated and banned 111 ingredients from over-the-counter diet pills, ruling them ineffective or potentially harmful, and cracked down on a wide range of products. However, it did not take a strong stance against phenyl-propanolamine (PPA) or benzocaine, two widely used ingredients in diet products.

Culminating a three-year investigation in the fall of 1993, the Federal Trade Commission charged five of the nation's largest commercial diet programs—Nutri/System, Jenny Craig, Weight Watchers, Physicians Weight Loss Centers, and Diet Center—with engaging in deceptive advertising by making unsubstantiated weight loss and weight loss maintenance claims, and by using consumer testimonials without proof that they represented the typical experience of the dieters on the programs. Allegations in some of the cases also addressed deceptive pricing, comparative superiority, rate of weight loss, or safety-related claims.

Jenny Craig and Weight Watchers are fighting the FTC charges, while Nutri/System, Diet Center, and Physicians Weight Loss Centers assented to settle under proposed consent agreements that include several provisions similar to those the FTC is seeking in litigation with the other two companies. These would prohibit the companies from misrepresenting the performance or safety of any weight loss program they offer in the future and would require them to have scientific data to back up future claims they make about weight loss and maintenance. Moreover, the FTC set out standards for the type of evidence that would be required to support various maintenance claims. For instance, statements that weight loss is maintained over the long term would have to be based on evidence of consumers followed for at least two years.

In addition, maintenance success claims in most ads would have to be accompanied by various clear and prominent disclosures, including the statement, "For many dieters, weight loss is temporary," as well as disclosures about the average weight loss maintenance for consumers on the relevant program. The disclosure as to average maintenance would not be required in broadcast ads of 30 seconds or shorter. However, the orders and settlements still would require those ads clearly to state, "For many dieters, weight loss is temporary," and that consumers should check with the companies for details about their maintenance records. They would be required to give potential consumers a written document containing maintenance data.

Moreover, the FTC's proposed orders and settlements would require any testimonials the respondents use to represent the results customers generally achieve, unless the companies also clearly and prominently disclose either the generally expected results or a statement such as, "This result is not typical. You may be less successful.". . .

Bolder Steps

Despite government enforcement, there is no doubt that the commercial weight loss industry will continue to prey on consumers and reap enormous profits. This is because the diet industry's advertising and marketing strategy is based on the creation and perpetuation of fear, biases, and stereotypes. Overweight persons are portrayed as unhealthy, unattractive, asexual, weak-willed, lazy, and gluttonous. Weight loss or a thin figure are equated with virtue, health, and success. Failure to participate in dieting or lack of success in losing weight are blamed on a lack of willpower, determination, or moral values. Fat people are taught to feel guilty and blame themselves for the failures of weight loss programs, and to expect and accept rejection, mistreatment, and discrimination regarding their weight. This negative image has a devastating impact on millions of fat people, as such messages lower their self-esteem and foster discontent, self-doubt, and self-hatred, especially during the weight regain phase of the dieting yo-yo cycle.

Because the diet industry preys on the low self-esteem and negative body image of both fat and average-size Americans, it will continue to profit, regardless of the caveats required by government regulation. Because consumers will continue to be seduced by advertising that sells them on dissatisfaction with their bodies, bolder steps must be taken.

Because of the biases of the medical community and the difficulty in isolating causes of death, fatalities caused by dieting often mistakenly are blamed on obesity. If doctors report deaths of known dieters, products or programs that are especially dangerous can be discovered sooner. To this end, the Centers for Disease Control should track the incidence of deaths of people who have followed a diet or used diet drugs or products within a year of their demise.

In order for consumers to make informed decisions about weight loss dieting and to help to end the social stigma and discrimination against fat people, a Federal labeling and advertising act that would ban radio and television commercials for weight loss diets and products should be enacted, similar to the 1971 Federal Cigarette Labelling and Advertising Act. In addition, warnings of a diet product's long-term ineffectiveness and possible health risks should be displayed clearly on all products, similar to the Surgeon General's warnings on cigarette packaging.

Government officials must take action. First, they must separate out the cultural bias against fat and the facts about obesity. Second, they must unravel the conflicts of interest that exist between the commercial weight loss industry and the obesity research community, members of which also serve as public health policymakers. Third, they must enact and enforce laws and regulations to protect both the public health and consumers' pocketbooks.

Periodical Bibliography

The following articles have been selected to supplement the diverse views presented in this chapter. Addresses are provided for periodicals not indexed in the *Readers' Guide to Periodical Literature*, the *Alternative Press Index*, or the *Social Sciences Index*.

Neal Barnard — "Eat All You Want and Lose Weight," *Natural Health*, July/August 1993. Available from 17 Station St., Brookline Village, MA 02147.

Patricia A. Brill and Kenneth H. Cooper — "Physical Exercise and Mental Health," *National Forum*, Winter 1993. Available from PO Box 16000, Louisiana State University, Baton Rouge, LA 70893.

Jane E. Brody — "For Most Trying to Lose Weight, Dieting Only Makes Things Worse," *New York Times*, November 23, 1992.

CQ Researcher — "Dieting and Health," April 14, 1995. Available from 1414 22nd St. NW, Washington, DC 20037.

Philip Elmer-Dewitt — "Fat Times," *Time*, January 16, 1995.

Peter Jaret — "The Old Advice: Work Out. The New Advice: Walk the Dog and Take the Stairs." *Health*, September 1994.

Janis Jibrin — "The Real Truth About Fat," *Glamour*, January 1994.

I-min Lee, Chung-cheng Hsieh, and Ralph S. Paffenbarger Jr. — "Exercise Intensity and Longevity in Men: The Harvard Alumni Health Study," *JAMA*, April 19, 1995. Available from 515 N. State St., Chicago, IL 60610.

Rudolph L. Leibel, Michael Rosenbaum, and Jules Hirsch — "Changes in Energy Expenditure Resulting from Altered Body Weight," *New England Journal of Medicine*, March 9, 1995. Available from 10 Shattuck St., Boston, MA 02115-6094.

Rita Rubin — "Fat and Fit," *U.S. News & World Report*, May 16, 1994.

Rita Rubin — "When Willpower Won't," *U.S. News & World Report*, May 15, 1995.

Leslie Vreeland — "Lean Times in Fat City," *Working Woman*, July 1995.

Are Alternative Therapies Viable?

*H*ealth
and
*F*itness

Chapter Preface

A 1993 study published in the *New England Journal of Medicine* revealed that one in three Americans have used alternative medicine to treat sprains or strains, allergies, arthritis, digestive problems, and many other ailments. These Americans spend almost fourteen billion dollars each year on acupuncture, biofeedback, massage therapy, and homeopathic remedies, among other treatments. Some health experts, including many physicians, are concerned about the use of these unconventional treatments. They fear that if sick people turn to alternative treatments so readily for relatively minor illnesses, they will also shun more established medical treatments for serious—even life-threatening—medical conditions. Physics professor Robert L. Park of the University of Maryland and biology professor Ursula Goodenough of Washington University argue, "To the extent that reliance on alternative therapies leads people to forgo valid medical treatment, it is dangerous."

Proponents of alternative medicine, however, disagree with this characterization of how it may be used. A 1991 study by Harvard Medical School's David M. Eisenberg indicates that chronic, not life-threatening, illnesses are the primary reason that patients use unconventional treatments and that 83 percent of those surveyed had first sought treatment for the same ailment from a mainstream physician. These proponents also maintain that many doctors, far from disapproving, are incorporating alternative therapies into their practices to help treat many problems that have resisted more standard efforts. Brian Berman, a family practitioner in Baltimore who is using some unconventional treatments to complement usual treatment, asserts: "I had great training for acute-care problems, but I didn't have a lot of the answers for chronic conditions. I started to look for other ways."

Insurance companies have begun to approve the use of many new treatments, so it appears that alternative therapies—whether ultimately beneficial or not—will continue to be readily available to consumers. The authors in the following chapter debate the viability of alternative medicine in general, as well as some specific treatments.

"Bolstered by mounting scientific evidence, some approaches once considered radical or 'alternative' are beginning to be viewed as 'complementary.'"

Some Alternative Therapies Are Valid

Marlene Cimons

In the following viewpoint, Marlene Cimons of the *Los Angeles Times* discusses a growing number of medical personnel who have turned to "alternative" medicine when more conventional approaches failed to alleviate problems—mostly chronic conditions—experienced by themselves and their patients. While few doctors can explain why or how these therapies work, Cimons writes, they are increasingly convinced that treatments such as osteopathy, homeopathy, and acupuncture will complement more mainstream treatment methods.

As you read, consider the following questions:

1. According to the author, what percentage of the world's health care services does the World Health Organization characterize as "alternative"?
2. How many Americans saw an alternative health care practitioner in 1990, according to Cimons?
3. Who is responsible for the shift in social attitudes toward using alternative therapies, according to the author?

Excerpted from Marlene Cimons, "New Life for Old Remedies," *Los Angeles Times*, January 1, 1996; ©1996, Los Angeles Times. Reprinted with permission.

When Dr. Brian Berman first saw him, the man's face was paralyzed by pain.

The 54-year-old cameraman suffered from trigeminal neuralgia, a condition that produces severe facial pain. He had found some relief through anesthetic nerve blocks and narcotic painkillers—but at a terrible price. He couldn't sleep, couldn't concentrate and was often depressed.

Berman decided to try something unconventional—indeed, something that many physicians once might have ridiculed: He prescribed belladonna, derived from a plant in the poisonous nightshade family. Within six months—using that drug and a second, causticum, made from a mineral—the pain receded by two-thirds, Berman said.

Today it is kept under control through such homeopathic drugs, supplemented by over-the-counter medications.

Combining Therapies

Berman, 45, a family medicine physician in Baltimore, began to combine "alternative" therapies with conventional treatments early in his practice.

"I had great training for acute-care problems, but I didn't have a lot of the answers for chronic conditions," he said. "I started to look for other ways."

Now many other doctors are beginning to do the same thing. They have discovered that integrating the unconventional with the mainstream not only can provide relief but also can do so with fewer side effects and without more invasive procedures, such as surgery.

"Complementary" Approaches to Medical Treatment

Bolstered by mounting scientific evidence, some approaches once considered radical or "alternative" are beginning to be viewed as "complementary."

Not all of the disciplines work for everyone. But as long as patients don't put their lives in jeopardy by rejecting established therapies, many physicians—even those most resistant to alternative medicine—now seem willing to take a second look.

Dr. Nancy Dickey is a family practice physician who chairs the board of trustees of the American Medical Association, a conservative doctors' organization long skeptical of alternative approaches. She reflected the new attitude when she acknowledged: "If I had a patient who said, 'I quit using codeine since I started doing acupuncture,' I'd say, 'Terrific.'"

According to the World Health Organization, 65% to 80% of the world's health care services can be classified as alternative—although the preferred term outside the United States is "traditional," since most of these approaches derive from ancient practices.

"These become complementary, alternative or unconventional when used in Western countries," said Dr. Wayne B. Jonas, director of the National Institutes of Health office of alternative medicine, which Congress established in 1992 to focus more scientific scrutiny on the field. "Even in countries where modern Western biomedicine dominates, the public makes extensive use of unconventional practices."

Complements to Modern Medicine

Western medicine is beginning to work side by side with Chinese medicine, as millions of people have come to view acupuncture and other forms of traditional medicine as complements to modern medicine. For example, a person with migraines may now see her medical doctor *and* an acupuncturist. A now-famous study published in the *New England Journal of Medicine* reported that "it is likely that virtually all medical doctors see patients who routinely use unconventional therapies."

Karen Baar, *Natural Health*, November/December 1994.

A 1990 study indicated that one in three Americans saw an alternative health care practitioner—ranging from osteopaths to acupuncturists—that year. More than 80% used them in conjunction with conventional medicine, according to the NIH.

It may be that Americans are turning to nonconventional medicine in record numbers because it represents "a simpler approach to healing than the high-tech medicine of the 20th century," said Dr. Thomas L. Delbanco, chief of general internal medicine at Boston's Beth Israel Hospital.

Seeking the "Good Old Days"

"People yearn for the 'good old days' when doctors spent more time listening to their patients than ordering complicated tests and procedures," Delbanco said. "This . . . is a response to modern life, where everything, including health care, often seems rushed and impersonal."

If so, doctors are beginning to listen. Jonas estimates that more than 50% of "conventional" physicians in the United States use or refer patients to these treatments. And medical schools are beginning to add training in alternative therapies to their curricula.

In addition, insurance companies, health maintenance organizations and other health plans have begun to cover alternative treatments, in part because they often cost less than standard procedures and also because customers want them.

"Consumers themselves are driving the change, and many of them are physicians who are themselves consumers," said Dr. James Gordon, chairman of the program advisory council of NIH's office on alternative medicine. "I've certainly seen physicians change because they had a health problem that was not helped by conventional therapy."

A Doctor Is a Believer

Gordon was one. A psychiatrist long interested in the therapeutic effects of alternative approaches, he became a believer after he seriously injured his lower back and was helped by an osteopath, who focuses on the musculoskeletal system's relationship to the body.

The most widely used alternative medicines—including homeopathy, acupuncture, Chinese herbs and mind-body approaches such as meditation and yoga—have long histories.

The NIH's Jonas points out that a new drug's average "half-life," or period of peak use, is about 20 years. Homeopathy has been around, unchanged, for almost 200 years; acupuncture for more than 2,000 years; prayer and spiritualism for at least 20,000 years. And "if one believes reports of monkeys using plant products to regulate their menstrual cycles," he said, "herbalism, probably the oldest, has been around for greater than 200,000 years."

Homeopathy, which originated in Europe in the early 1800s, is based on the idea of "like cures like." It involves treating a disease by giving highly diluted preparations of substances that actually *cause* the same symptoms.

Berman notes that similar treatments exist in conventional medicine, such as the drug digitalis, which controls heart irregularities when given in small doses and causes them when given in large ones.

Attests to Success

In homeopathy, "the medication is so diluted that there are no molecules left," Berman said, repeating a criticism voiced by skeptics for years. "So how can you have an action? I don't know. But I've seen it work."

There is more scientific understanding of acupuncture, which is derived from traditional Chinese medicine and used for pain control and other disorders. It involves the use of whisper-thin needles inserted into the skin at specific points. Stimulating these points alters chemical neurotransmitters in the body. . . .

Acceptance Predicted

Berman predicts it will take another decade for society to undergo a major transformation in the way it views alternative therapies. It will happen after enough scientific evidence accumulates to support largely anecdotal success stories.

"From my perspective, we're not talking about conventional vs. complementary, but effective vs. noneffective," Berman said. "That is what will take us away from this we-versus-them attitude."

"To the extent that reliance on alternative therapies leads people to forgo valid medical treatment, it is dangerous."

Alternative Therapies Are Not Valid

Robert L. Park and Ursula Goodenough

Robert L. Park is a professor of physics at the University of Maryland at College Park. Ursula Goodenough is a professor of biology at Washington University in St. Louis. In the following viewpoint, Park and Goodenough contend that the federal government's creation of the Office of Alternative Medicine at the National Institutes of Health has fostered the mistaken belief among both physicians and laypeople that alternative treatments are viable. The authors maintain that there is still no scientific evidence to support the use of alternative therapies and that these therapies may actually be dangerous if they supplant necessary medical treatment for severe illness.

As you read, consider the following questions:

1. What criticisms do the authors level against the National Institutes of Health's Office of Alternative Medicine?
2. According to Park and Goodenough, why do health maintenance organizations find alternative therapies appealing?
3. What specific alternative treatments do the authors discuss, and how do they characterize each one of the treatments?

Robert L. Park and Ursula Goodenough, "Buying Snake Oil with Tax Dollars," *New York Times*, January 3, 1996, p. A11. Copyright ©1996 by The New York Times Company. Reprinted by permission.

It goes by different names now—biofield therapeutics, mental healing, homeopathy—but magic has been used to treat the sick throughout history. The shaman shakes his rattles, the faith healer lays on hands—sometimes patients die, some make surprising recoveries. The only thing that has changed is that the "healers" of today apparently have the endorsement of the National Institutes of Health.

The Office of Alternative Medicine

In 1992, Congress directed the N.I.H. to create an Office of Alternative Medicine to evaluate "unconventional medical practices." Scientists hoped that the office would have a mandate to debunk superstition masquerading as science. Unfortunately, so-called alternative medicine has come to be cloaked in a mantle of N.I.H. respectability.

The office poses little financial threat to other biomedical research: the N.I.H. spends only about $14 million of its $11 billion annual budget on alternative medicine. But its impact on health policy is greatly out of proportion to the size of its budget.

The new respectability accorded to alternative medicine was evident at a recent conference on relaxation and spiritual healing in Boston, where representatives of health maintenance organizations mingled with snake handlers and spiritual healers. Alternative techniques appeal to H.M.O.'s because they are far cheaper than traditional medicine.

The Federal Government is not alone in buying into miracle cures. King County, Washington, recently established the nation's first government-subsidized "naturopathic" health clinic.

Health sections in newspapers and television news programs are filled with sensational accounts of amazing health benefits from touch therapy, spiritual healing and a dozen other remedies that were once the stuff of tabloids. The accounts tend toward new-age techno-babble about "universal energy" and "vortexes," and testimonials from grateful recipients. Often someone from the Office of Alternative Medicine is quoted as saying the therapy is "interesting" or "worthy of study"—rarely is there a hint of scientific skepticism.

Is It Science?

The real question is not whether alternative medicine is good science but whether it is science at all.

Consider so-called touch therapy. The therapist's hands do not actually touch the patient; instead, they smooth out the "energy field" or "aura" surrounding the body. As with the emperor's new clothes, only the therapist can detect this aura. No evidence of this energy has ever been offered, yet touch therapy is being practiced in hospitals across the country.

Practitioners of homeopathy say they treat patients with "natural" substances such as minerals and organic extracts. But the active ingredients in homeopathic medicines are usually so diluted that the chance of even one molecule of the substance remaining in a solution is less than one in a billion. Advocates claim that it doesn't matter, that the water "remembers" the ingredient and retains its supposed healing powers.

Quackery

Promoters of quackery are adept at using slogans and buzzwords. During the 1970s, they popularized the word "natural" as a magic sales slogan. During the 80s, the word "holistic" gained similar use. Today's leading buzzword is "alternative." Correctly employed, it refers to methods that have equal value for a particular purpose. (An example would be two antibiotics capable of killing a particular organism.) When applied to unproven methods, however, the term can be misleading because methods that are unsafe or ineffective are not reasonable alternatives to proven treatments.

Stephen Barrett, *Priorities*, Spring 1993.

Shark cartilage, widely sold as a cure for cancer, can be ingested orally or by enema. Yet the alleged active ingredient is a protein, and proteins do not cross the lining of the intestines into the body.

Few Benefits

This is not to say that some patients do not benefit from some alternative practices. To the extent that the treatment offers hope, comfort or relief from stress, alternative medicines can reduce blood pressure and release pain-relieving endorphins.

If this placebo effect sometimes works, why should we worry about the spread of such techniques? After all, no one has ever been harmed by having his aura manipulated.

Giving a Federal imprimatur to such techniques invites deception. The licensing procedures and scrutiny that the medical profession imposes on itself are not relevant in evaluating treatments that depend on belief. We can joke about people selling snake oil, but some are making a great deal of money selling it. About $13 billion per year is spent by Americans on alternative treatments, many of which have no scientific basis. The money aside, to the extent that reliance on alternative therapies leads people to forgo valid medical treatment, it is dangerous.

There is an even more insidious problem. Biomedical research (much of it financed by the N.I.H.) is on a spectacular roll, with important new insights emerging daily. These gains, however, can alienate those who want to believe that events are not determined solely by physical laws. There is nostalgia for a time when things seemed simpler and more natural. The attention given alternative treatments can lead people to overlook that genes, enzymes, hormones and antibodies are natural.

Should there be an Office of Alternative Medicine to evaluate unconventional practices? Not one that elevates magical notions to matters of serious scientific debate. Scientists cannot afford to spend their time and taxpayers' money testing every unlikely claim.

Magic or Science

Humans love to believe that magic charms our lives. In many ways it does, as in the magic of love or kindness or sunsets. But it is important to distinguish these experiences from claims that ignore natural law. Scientific understanding of nature can expose charlatans and lead to the development of valid therapies. In the process, we experience the magic of awe and reverence as we come to understand how nature really works.

"[Homeopathy] has an impressive track record."

Homeopathic Remedies Are Beneficial

Nancy Bruning

Homeopathy, an old-fashioned way of treating illness by using minute quantities of herbs diluted in water or grain alcohol, has regained support in natural health circles. In the following viewpoint, Nancy Bruning asserts that while neither believers nor skeptics can explain how it works, homeopathy can successfully treat a wide range of health problems, from anxiety to coughs to sore muscles to insomnia. Bruning is a health and environment writer and the author of *Healing Homeopathic Remedies*.

As you read, consider the following questions:

1. How did the American Medical Association affect the practice of homeopathy in the nineteenth century, according to Bruning?
2. What are the rules that Bruning cites for taking homeopathic remedies?
3. According to the author, how do most homeopaths view the relationship between homeopathy and other healing methods?

Nancy Bruning, "The Mysterious Power of Homeopathy," *Natural Health*, January/February 1995. Reprinted with permission. For a trial issue of *Natural Health*, call 1-800-526-8440.

Forget the skeptics—even practitioners of homeopathy struggle to explain this bizarre but seemingly effective system of healing. This is not surprising given that homeopathy defies the known laws of chemistry, physics, and pharmacology. For starters, homeopathic medicines contain substances known to cause the symptoms you want to eliminate. Imagine taking poison ivy pills to relieve itching.

And if that isn't enough, the homeopathic preparations are made by repeatedly diluting the active ingredient—putting an ounce of the ingredient in ten ounces of water, then an ounce of that dilution in ten ounces of water, and so on—until it's unlikely that even a single molecule of the active ingredient will be present in the dose you take. Moreover, the more dilute the preparation, the more potent it is considered to be. All this combines to throw skeptic and believer alike into a baffling realm of theory and speculation where matter dissolves into pure energy, where small permutations in a system can create large changes, and where wave patterns and electromagnetic messages affect not only the body and mind but even the spirit.

Naturally, most scientists scoff at claims that homeopathy can relieve illness. What they can't do, however, is ignore the many people who swear that it can. My own experience a few years ago landed me in the ranks of the believers. When my yoga instructor recommended a popular homeopathic remedy, Calmes Forté, for my insomnia; I tried it, and it worked. Also, I had no druggy feeling the next day, as I might have had with sleeping pills. Over the next several months it continued to work more often than not. But like most people who use homeopathic medicines, I hadn't a clue as to why.

Two years later, I teamed up with a physician trained in homeopathic medicine—Corey Weinstein—and wrote a book about homeopathy. It was then that I learned that this system has an impressive track record and is supported with increasing frequency by publications in scientific journals.

In fact, homeopathy was the medicine of choice for many nineteenth-century American physicians. In the 1850s, however, the newly formed American Medical Association began to rout homeopathy from the halls of "respected" medicine. At the turn of the century there were 15,000 practicing homeopaths in the United States (15 to 20 percent of the entire medical profession), but by the 1970s fewer than 200 practitioners remained.

Now, homeopathy is on the rebound. A survey published in the *New England Journal of Medicine* found that 2.3 million Americans used homeopathy in 1990, and the National Center for Homeopathy estimates that at least 2,500 practitioners use homeopathy in the United States. Sales of homeopathic medicines in health and drug stores are rising at the rate of 25 percent annually as people use these medicines to treat themselves for a variety of problems.

How Homeopathy Works

There is a principle of homeopathy called the Law of Similars, which holds that "like cures like." This means that a substance that causes certain symptoms in a healthy person can, when given in infinitesimal doses, cure those same symptoms in a sick person. For example, consider the homeopathic remedy *Coffea*. It's made from coffee, well-known for its ability to cause jumpiness and wakefulness. As a remedy, however, *Coffea* is prescribed to calm your nerves and help you sleep. Similarly, *Allium cepa*, which is made from onions, relieves the symptoms of watery eyes and runny nose.

In homeopathy, symptoms are seen neither as enemies to be squashed nor as the disease itself. "Rather," says Dana Ullman, president of the Foundation for Homeopathic Research in Berkeley, California, "they are signs of the body's effort to deal with infection or stress, to defend and heal. Because our bodies are not always completely effective in healing, giving a substance that mimics the body's defense helps trigger that process."

Homeopaths maintain that while suppressing symptoms outright may help you feel better temporarily, it won't help the healing process. In one of the many analogies that homeopaths use to explain their system, countering symptoms with "anti"-histamines or "anti"-biotics is said to be like smashing a beeping smoke alarm instead of looking for the fire that set it off.

Unlike a smoke alarm, however, symptoms are part of the healing process. For instance, even conventional medicine now recognizes that fever helps the body fight infection and that a runny nose clears the body of mucus and dead pathogens.

Homeopaths believe that although symptoms may be unpleasant, they play an important role in healing, and therefore should be stimulated and supported rather than suppressed. Only then can the body rid itself of disease and return to health; the symptoms will fade away naturally when they are no longer needed. Ullman likens homeopathy to "steering *into* a skid" to regain control of your car, rather than steering against the direction of the skid, which only sends you further out of control.

You can take one of two basic categories of homeopathic remedies: *combination* remedies or *single* remedies. Combination remedies include two or more of the single remedies that are most likely to alleviate specific symptoms, such as a cough, indigestion, or muscle aches. Single homeopathic remedies are specific to an individual's overall pattern of symptoms, which in the case of a cough, for example, may include whether the person feels hot or cold, what time of day the cough is worst, and how dry or wet the cough is. Since people's overall symptom patterns will differ, two people with a cough may require different single remedies. Thus, combination remedies are more likely to contain the remedy you will need. For people without experience in homeopathy, they are much easier to use than single remedies.

Picking the Right Remedy

Homeopathic Products

Conditions	Aconite	Apis	Arnica	Arsenicum	Belladonna	Bryonia	Carbo veg.	Chamomilla	Ferrum phos.	Gelsemium	Hepar sulph.	Ipecac	Mercurius	Nux vomica	Phosphorus	Pulsatilla	Rhus tox.	Sulphur
Acne				X									X				X	X
Anxiety	X									X				X	X			
Backache			X											X			X	X
Bruises, Sprains & Strains			X											X			X	X
Coughs & Cold	X							X	X						X			
Depression								X					X				X	X
Eczema				X							X						X	X
Exhaustion			X				X			X			X					
Gas				X			X	X					X					
Headache	X				X	X				X								
Indigestion							X					X	X			X		
Insomnia								X			X		X			X		
Irritability		X												X	X	X		
Neck Stiffness	X					X							X				X	
PMS								X						X			X	X
Sinusitis					X					X	X					X		
Toothache					X			X					X			X		

Nancy Bruning, *Natural Health*, January/February 1995.

Combination remedies are used mainly for acute (sudden onset, short-lived) conditions which have simpler and more consistent symptom patterns than chronic (slower developing, longer-lasting) conditions. Acute conditions include minor injuries and wounds, insect bites, burns and sunburn, and muscle strains and sprains. You can also use combination remedies to treat yourself pre- and post-operatively to help deal with shock and to speed healing. And they are often used successfully to fight flus, colds, coughs, and sore throats; headaches and hangovers; digestive problems such as nausea, vomiting, diarrhea, and constipation; and kids' problems, such as earaches, teething pain, and toothaches. A correct combination remedy can even soothe acute emotional reactions such as fear and anxiety before an exam, performance, or other big event.

Brands of combination remedies vary as to the remedies they contain, and although this "shotgun" approach increases the chance a product will contain the remedy you need, it doesn't guarantee it. So if you don't get relief from one particular combination, you may need to try other brands until you find the one that works. If you still fail to see any benefits, don't give up on homeopathy altogether—the combinations you've tried may not contain the particular remedy you require. For another ailment, or at another time, the same or another product may work wonderfully. Also, you may need to find a homeopathic specialist who will help you find the correct single remedy needed for your symptoms.

Constitutional Remedies

Single remedies (sometimes called constitutional remedies) are often necessary for chronic conditions that have endured for months, years, or your whole life, and which may be more deep-seated and complicated. Choosing the correct single remedy requires some study and perhaps a little luck on the part of the patient, or the skill and expertise of a professional homeopath.

Constitutional homeopathy can often help cure such chronic conditions as acne, allergies, migraine headaches, asthma, depression, anxiety, fatigue, premenstrual syndrome, arthritis, eczema, and psoriasis. Professionally guided constitutional therapy is also recommended if you want to go beyond self-care and cure the underlying disease that may be at the root of recurring acute symptoms.

While combination remedies tend to be easier to use, some homeopaths, such as Jennifer Jacobs, M.D., a family physician in Seattle, encourage people to at least try self-prescribing single remedies for acute conditions. If chosen correctly, they are more effective than the combinations because they are used in higher potencies and are more specific to the individual. However, you can't just wander into a store and expect to choose the right single remedy off the shelf. The playing field can be confusing to the novice, in part because manufacturers label single remedies with just a few parts of the total symptom profile. . . .

Rules for Homeopathy

Homeopathy comes with its own set of rules to follow for taking remedies. Some—such as caveats against touching the remedy or drinking coffee—may seem illogical to the average person. And, admittedly there are differences of opinion within the profession as to how strictly you need to observe these rules. However, the consensus is that to be safe and to give homeopathy the best chance of working, it's advisable to follow these guidelines:

1. The frequency of the dosage depends on the intensity of the symptoms. Severe symptoms that come on suddenly, such as earache, may require a dose every five minutes; a slowly developing flu may need the remedy every three or four hours. As the symptoms improve or disappear, increase the interval between doses or stop the medication. Start again if the same symptoms return. However, if there has been no response to the remedy after six doses, switch to another remedy.

2. Avoid touching the remedy with your hands. Instead, tip the required number of pellets into the container cap and from the cap into your mouth; if the tablets are blister-packed, pop them directly into your mouth. Homeopaths say that touching the remedy could contaminate it or inactivate it.

3. Avoid eating or drinking anything but chlorine-free water for fifteen to thirty minutes before and after taking the remedy. And allow the remedy to dissolve slowly under your tongue so it is absorbed directly into the tiny sublingual capillaries. (Some combination tablets include instructions to chew them.)

4. Store homeopathic remedies in their original containers, away from heat and sunlight. Also, keep them away from strong-smelling substances that might contaminate them, such as perfumes, camphor, and eucalyptus. (These and other aromatic substances are found in items that inhabit the medicine chest.) Some homeopaths also advise against drinking herbal teas or ingesting products containing mint (for instance, toothpaste) within a half-hour of taking remedies.

5. Avoid drinking coffee during treatment. Coffee may counteract the remedy's effect by acting as an antidote or by otherwise slowing the healing process.

Another area of debate among homeopaths is the relationship of homeopathic treatment to other forms of medicine. Some homeopaths feel that all you really need to treat an illness is the right homeopathic remedy. However, most say that other natural healing methods help when used appropriately, and that conventional medicine also has its place. Most homeopaths stress the importance of good health habits such as proper diet, exercise, rest, vacation time, satisfying social relationships, creative living, effective stress management, and spiritual nourishment. Since the goal of homeopathy is to stimulate the body's ability to heal, it makes sense to support the body's efforts with healthy living.

"If the FDA required homeopathic remedies to be proven effective in order to remain on the market . . . homeopathy would face extinction in the United States."

Homeopathic Remedies Are a Fraud

Stephen Barrett

Homeopathic remedies were widely used in the nineteenth century, when they were less dangerous than many standard medical practices, Stephen Barrett maintains in the following viewpoint. However, Barrett contends that those who use homeopathic remedies now should be aware that they are largely unregulated by the federal government and are therefore potentially harmful. He also asserts that the herbal solutions are impotent because they are so dilute that none of the original herb remains. Barrett is a long-time consumer advocate and the author of more than thirty-five books dealing with consumer health issues, including *The Health Robbers: A Close Look at Quackery in America.*

As you read, consider the following questions:

1. According to the author, why are homeopathic remedies legally marketable as drugs?
2. What are homeopathy's historical roots, according to Barrett?
3. What is the process for making homeopathic remedies, as described by Barrett?

Excerpted from Stephen Barrett, "Homeopathy's Legacy: Phony 'Remedies' and Kindred Delusions," Quackwatch, *Priorities*, vol. 6, no. 1, pp. 13–17. Reprinted by permission of the American Council on Science and Health.

Homeopathic "remedies" enjoy a unique status in the health marketplace: they are the only quack products legally marketable as drugs. This situation is the result of two circumstances. First, the 1938 Federal Food, Drug, and Cosmetic Act, which was shepherded through Congress by a homeopathic physician who was also a senator, recognizes as drugs all substances included in the *Homeopathic Pharmacopeia of the United States*. Second, the FDA [Food and Drug Administration] has not required proof that homeopathic remedies work.

Basic Misbeliefs

Homeopathy dates back to the late 1700s when Samuel Hahnemann (1755–1843), a German physician, began formulating its basic principles. Hahnemann was justifiably distressed about bloodletting, leeching, purging and other medical procedures of his day that did far more harm than good. Thinking that these treatments were intended to "balance the body's 'humors' by opposite effects," he developed his "law of similars"—a notion that symptoms of disease can be cured by substances that produce similar symptoms in healthy people. The word "homeopathy" is derived from the Greek words *homeo* (similar) and *pathos* (suffering or disease).

Hahnemann and his early followers conducted "provings" in which they administered herbs, minerals and other substances to healthy people, including themselves, and kept detailed records of what they observed. Later these records were compiled into lengthy reference books called *materia medica*, which are used to match a patient's symptoms with a "corresponding" drug.

Hahnemann declared that diseases represent a disturbance in the body's ability to heal itself and that only a small stimulus is needed to begin the healing process. At first he used small doses of accepted medications. But later he used enormous dilutions and theorized that the smaller the dose, the more powerful the effect—a principle he called the "law of infinitesimals." That, of course, is just the opposite of what pharmacologists have demonstrated. Moreover, if it were true, every substance encountered by a molecule of water might imprint an "essence" that could exert powerful (and unpredictable) medicinal effects when ingested by a person.

The basis for inclusion in the *Homeopathic Pharmacopeia* is not modern scientific testing, but homeopathic "provings" conducted as long as 150 years ago. The current (ninth) edition describes how more than a thousand substances are prepared for homeopathic use. It does not identify the symptoms or diseases for which homeopathic products should be used; that is determined by the practitioner.

Homeopathic products are made from minerals, botanical substances, zoological substances and several other sources. If the medicinal substance is soluble, one part is diluted with either nine or 99 parts of distilled water and/or alcohol and shaken vigorously; if insoluble, it is finely ground and pulverized in similar proportions with powdered lactose (milk sugar). The process is then repeated until the desired concentration is reached. Dilutions of one to ten are designated by the Roman numeral X (1X = 1/10, 3X = 1/1,000, 6X = 1/1,000,000). Similarly, dilutions of one to 100 are designated by the Roman numeral C (1C = 1/100, 3C = 1/1,000,000 and so on). Most remedies today range from 6X to 30X.

Pseudoscience

A pseudoscience based on the idea that symptoms can be cured by taking infinitesimal amounts of substances that, in larger amounts, can produce similar symptoms in healthy people. Homeopathic therapy states that the more dilute the remedy, the more powerful it is. The FDA has tolerated the marketing of homeopathic remedies without requiring that they be proven effective like other drugs.

Joseph C. Elia, *Manchester Union Leader*, August 18, 1993.

According to the laws of chemistry, there is a limit to the dilution that can be made without losing the original substance altogether. This limit, the reciprocal of Avogadro's number (6.023 x 10^{23}), corresponds to homeopathic potencies of 12C or 24X (one part in 10^{24}). Hahnemann himself realized there is virtually no chance that even one molecule of original substance would remain after extreme dilutions. But he believed that the vigorous shaking or pulverizing with each step of dilution leaves behind a "spirit-like" essence—"no longer perceptible to the senses"—which cures by reviving the body's "vital force." This notion is utter nonsense.

The Decline of Homeopathy

Because homeopathic remedies were actually less dangerous than those of nineteenth-century medical orthodoxy, many medical practitioners began using them. But as medical science and medical education advanced, homeopathy declined sharply, particularly in America, where its schools have either closed or converted to modern methods.

In 1986, I sent a questionnaire to the deans of all 72 U.S. pharmacy schools. Faculty members from 49 schools responded. Most said their school either didn't mention homeopathy at all or considered it of historical interest only. Hahnemann's "law of similars" did not find a single supporter, and all but one respondent said his "law of infinitesimals" was wrong also. Almost all said that homeopathic remedies were neither potent nor effective, except possibly as placebos for mild, self-limiting ailments. About half felt that homeopathic remedies should be completely removed from the marketplace.

In 1987, *Consumer Reports* stated:

> Unless the laws of chemistry have gone awry, most homeopathic remedies are too diluted to have any physiological effect. . . . Any system of medicine embracing the use of such remedies involves a potential danger to patients whether the prescribers are M.D.s, other licensed practitioners, or outright quacks. Ineffective drugs are dangerous drugs when used to treat serious or life-threatening disease. Moreover . . . using them for a serious illness or undiagnosed pain instead of obtaining proper medical attention could prove harmful or even fatal.

Hype for Sale

Homeopathic remedies are available from practitioners, health-food stores and drugstores and manufacturers who sell directly to the public. Products are also sold person-to-person through multilevel marketing companies. Several companies sell home-remedy kits. The size of the homeopathic marketplace is unknown because the largest manufacturers keep their sales figures private. However, *Health Foods Business* estimated that 1992 sales through health-food stores totaled about $160 million.

A 1991 survey by the National Board of Chiropractic Examiners (NBCE) found that 36.9 percent of 4,835 full-time chiropractic practitioners who responded said that they had prescribed homeopathic remedies within the previous two years. The 1993 directory of the National Center for Homeopathy (NCH) in Alexandria, Virginia, lists about 300 licensed practitioners, about half of them physicians and the rest mostly naturopaths, chiropractors, acupuncturists, veterinarians, dentists, nurses or physician's assistants. Although several hundred physicians and naturopaths not listed in the NCH directory practice homeopathy to some extent, they appear to be greatly outnumbered by chiropractors.

Practicing Homeopathy

Homeopathic physicians who follow Hahnemann's methods closely take an elaborate history to "fit the remedy to the individual." The history typically includes standard medical questions plus many more about such things as emotions, moods, food preferences and reactions to the weather. A remedy is then selected with the help of a *materia medica* or computer program. Other practitioners, whose approaches have not been systematically tabulated, may spend little time with patients. In the 1992 *Digest of Chiropractic Economics*, for example, a chiropractor who runs a homeopathic manufacturing company described how he had treated a patient with a history of hay fever; allergies to dust, mold and animals; frequent sinusitis, constant postnasal drip; frequent cough; cold hands and feet; skipped heart beats; unhealthy skin; insomnia; abdominal bloating; and slowness in healing skin sores. The bill for eleven visits totaling 107 minutes came to $1,007.24.

A few practitioners who consider themselves homeopaths use "electrodiagnostic" devices to help select the remedies they prescribe. These devices—some of which have been seized by enforcement agencies—are little more than fancy galvanometers that measure electrical resistance of the patient's skin when touched by a probe. But these practitioners claim that the instruments detect disease by measuring disturbances in the body's flow of "electromagnetic energy."

Homeopathic Remedies Are Underregulated

Federal laws and regulations require that drugs be safe, effective and properly labeled for their intended use. However, the FDA has not applied this framework to most homeopathic remedies. A recent article in a health-food industry trade publication said: "There is more freedom in selling homeopathy than most other categories." Another article even suggested that "when a customer comes into your store complaining of an earache, fever, flu, sore throat, diarrhea or some other common health problem . . . one word that should immediately come out of your mouth is 'homeopathy.'" A third article said that, because of an FDA crackdown on several nutritional supplements, "more and more companies were turning to herbs and homeopathy to regain sales." Yet another article stated: "Homeopathy is natural medicine's favorite son in the 1990s. Suddenly the category is appearing everywhere—in newspapers, on radio talk shows, on special television programs. . . . For natural products retailers, it can be a dream come true."

A few companies encourage health professionals to prescribe their products for serious diseases. In 1983, Biological Homeopathic Industries (BHI) of Albuquerque, New Mexico, sent a 123-page catalog to almost 200,000 physicians nationwide. Among its products were *BHI Anticancer Stimulating, BHI Antivirus, BHI Stroke* and fifty other types of tablets claimed to be effective against serious diseases. In 1984, the FDA forced the company to stop distributing several of the products and to tone down its claims for the rest. However, the company's publishing arm issues the quarterly *Biological Therapy: Journal of Natural Medicine*, which regularly contains articles whose authors make questionable claims. An article in the April 1993 issue, for example, listed "indications" for using BHI and Heel products (distributed by BHI) for more than fifty conditions—including cancer, angina pectoris and paralysis. And the October 1993 issue, devoted to the homeopathic treatment of children, includes an article recommending products for acute bacterial infections of the ear and tonsils. The article is described as selections from Heel seminars given in several cities by a Nevada homeopath who also serves as medical editor of *Biological Therapy*.

Homeopathy in the Media

The National Center for Homeopathy keeps close track of homeopathy's portrayal by the media. Its September, October and November 1993 newsletters rated 75 articles and broadcasts and concluded that 57 articles (76 percent) were favorable, 13 articles (17 percent) were unfavorable and five articles (seven percent) were neutral. Most reports simply parrot the claims of homeopathy's promoters.

In the United States, homeopathy's most prolific publicist is probably Dana Ullman, M.P.H., president of the Foundation for Homeopathic Education and Research. At a recent meeting, Ullman informed me that his foundation, despite its name, does not fund research because he does not have sufficient time for fundraising. Nature's Way, of Springville, Utah, is now marketing over-the-counter products formulated by Ullman. The products include: *Insomnia, Sinusitis, Migraine Headache; Vaginitis, Menopause* (for women), and *Earache* (for children). The company has promised an "aggressive marketing strategy"—with ads in health-care, women's and parenting magazines—intended to "make homeopathy a household word." Its ads claim that "homeopathic medicine offers a significant advantage over its orthodox counterparts." Other companies have marketed such products as *Arthritis Formula, Bleeding, Kidney Disorders, Flu, Herpes, Exhaustion, Whooping Cough, Gonorrhea, Heart Tonic, Gall-Stones, Prostate Pain, Candida Yeast Infection, Cardio Forte, Thyro Forte, Worms* and *Smoking Withdrawal Tablets*.

Unimpressive "Research"

Since many homeopathic remedies contain no detectable amount of active ingredient, it is impossible to test whether they contain what their label says. Unlike most potent drugs, they have not been proven effective against disease by double-blind testing.

In 1990, an article in *Review of Epidemiology* analyzed 40 randomized trials that compared homeopathic treatment with standard treatment, a placebo or no treatment. The authors concluded that all but three of the trials had major flaws in their design and that only one of those three had reported a positive result. The authors concluded that there was no evidence that homeopathic treatment has any more value than a placebo.

Proponents trumpet the few "positive" studies as proof that "homeopathy works." Even if their results can be consistently reproduced (which seems unlikely), the most that the study of a single remedy for a single disease could prove is that the remedy is effective against that disease. It would not validate homeopathy's basic theories or prove that homeopathic treatment is useful for other diseases. . . .

Not Proven Effective

Homeopaths are working hard to have their services covered in the new health care reform proposals. They claim to provide care that is safer, gentler, "natural," less expensive than conventional care—and more concerned with prevention. I find the "prevention" claim particularly odious because homeopathic treatments prevent nothing and many homeopathic leaders preach against immunization.

If the FDA required homeopathic remedies to be proven effective in order to remain on the market—the standard it applies to other remedies—homeopathy would face extinction in the United States. However, there is no indication that the agency is considering this. FDA officials regard homeopathy as relatively benign and believe that other problems should get enforcement priority. If the FDA attacks homeopathy too vigorously, its proponents might even persuade Congress to rescue them. Regardless of this risk, the FDA should not permit worthless products to be marketed with claims that they are effective.

"Many effects of meditation seem beneficial and research suggests that it can be therapeutic for various psychological and psychosomatic disorders."

Meditation Promotes Well-Being

Roger Walsh

Roger Walsh is a professor of psychiatry, philosophy, and anthropology at the University of California at Irvine. In the following viewpoint, Walsh asserts that meditation, although the subject of little scientific research, appears to reduce stress and enhance well-being. Reducing stress through meditation, Walsh suggests, can improve some health problems, including high blood pressure, asthma, migraine, and high cholesterol.

As you read, consider the following questions:

1. What types of experiences can emerge during meditation, according to Walsh?
2. According to Walsh, how can meditation affect the cardiovascular system?
3. What psychological disorders does meditation alleviate, according to the author?

Excerpted from Roger Walsh, "State of the Art: An Overview of Research on Meditation," *Noetic Sciences Review*, Spring 1993. This article was adapted from *Paths Beyond Ego: The Transpersonal Vision*, edited by Roger Walsh and Frances Vaughan, and is reprinted with permission from The Putnam Publishing Group/Jeremy P. Tarcher, Inc. Copyright © 1993 by Roger Walsh and Frances Vaughan.

Meditation has been practiced for some 4000 years and perhaps even longer. Yet for most of that time, research consisted solely of personal, subjective experimentation by practitioners. Objective scientific research in the West began only in the twentieth century. Initial experiments tested claims of spectacular physiological feats by yogis, and additional research was initiated in the late sixties. However the variables examined have often been relatively gross and tangential to the subtle transpersonal shifts in awareness, emotions and values that constitute the traditional goals of meditation.

Effects of Meditation: Psychological

The range of experiences that can emerge during meditation is enormous. Experiences may be pleasant or painful and intense, and overwhelming emotions such as love or anger can alternate with periods of calm and equanimity. Although the idea of meditation as a simple relaxation response is a vast oversimplification, the general trend as practice continues is toward greater calm, positive emotions, and perceptual and introspective sensitivity. Experiences of advanced meditators include profound peace, concentration and joy, intense positive emotions of love and compassion, penetrating insights into the nature of mind, and a variety of transcendent states that can run the gamut of classical mystical experiences.

To date most knowledge of meditative experiences has come from personal accounts and there has been little systematic phenomenological research. However, there have been a large number of experimental studies of meditation's effects on personality, performance, and perception.

A fascinating pilot study of perception examined the Rorschach test responses of Buddhist meditators ranging from beginners to enlightened masters. Beginners showed normal response patterns whereas subjects with greater concentration saw, not the usual images such as animals and people, but simply the patterns of light and dark on the Rorschach cards. That is, their minds showed little tendency to elaborate these patterns into organized images, a finding consistent with the claim that concentration focuses the mind and reduces the number of associations.

Buddhist Enlightenment

Further striking findings characterized subjects who had reached the first of the four classic stages of Buddhist enlightenment. At first glance their Rorschachs were not obviously different from those of nonmeditators. However these subjects viewed the images they saw as creations of their own minds and were aware of the moment-by-moment process by which their stream of consciousness became organized into images.

Interestingly, subjects who had reached the first stage of enlightenment displayed evidence of normal conflicts around issues such as dependency, sexuality and aggression. However, they showed remarkably little defensiveness and reactivity to these conflicts. In other words, they accepted and were unperturbed by their neuroses.

Those few meditators who had reached the most advanced stages of enlightenment gave reports that were unique in three ways. First, these meditation masters saw not only the images but the ink blot itself as a projection of mind. Second, they showed no evidence of drive conflicts and appeared free of psychological conflicts usually considered an inescapable part of human existence. This finding is consistent with classic claims that psychological suffering can be dramatically reduced in advanced stages of meditation.

Mind-Body Medicine

Mind-body medicine tells us that expressing emotions (negative or positive), talking, meditating, even touching, can make a tremendous difference in our *physical* as well as emotional, well-being. Consider the evidence.

In Boston, Jon Kabat-Zinn has taught more than 6,000 people how to control stress and pain through meditation. Three-fourths of his patients report improvement in their condition after a year. . . .

At the University of California at San Francisco, Dean Ornish has shown for the first time that coronary heart disease actually can be reversed without drugs or surgery. Ornish's patients follow a low-fat diet and an exercise regimen, plus a program to reduce stress that includes yoga, meditation and group support. At the end of a year, 82 percent had improved blood flow to the heart and clearer arteries.

Bill Moyers, *USA Weekend*, February 5-7, 1993.

Third, these masters systematically linked their responses to all ten Rorschach cards into an integrated response on a single theme. The result was a systematic teaching about the nature of human suffering and its alleviation. In other words, the meditation masters transformed the Rorschach testing into a teaching for the testers!

Other studies show evidence for enhanced creativity, perceptual sensitivity, empathy, lucid dreaming, self-actualization, a positive sense of self-control, and marital satisfaction. Studies of

Transcendental Meditation (TM) suggest that it may foster maturation as measured by scales of ego, moral and cognitive development, intelligence, academic achievement, self-actualization and states of consciousness.

Physiological Variables

Physiological research began with sporadic investigations of spectacular yogic feats such as altering body temperature and heart rate. When some of these claims proved valid, more systematic investigation was begun.

For example, initial studies of metabolic effects reported marked reductions in metabolic rate—as shown by reduced oxygen consumption, carbon dioxide production, and blood lactate levels—and suggested that Transcendental Meditation led to a unique hypometabolic state. Subsequent studies confirmed a reduced metabolic rate but the introduction of better controls led to the recognition that many physiological effects initially assumed to be unique to meditation could actually be induced by other self-control strategies such as relaxation, biofeedback or self-hypnosis. This led some researchers to assume prematurely that there is little that is unique to meditation or its effects, an issue that is still being actively explored.

The Benefits of Meditation

The cardiovascular system is clearly affected. During meditation, heart rate drops, and with regular practice blood pressure also falls. Meditation can therefore be a useful treatment for mild high blood pressure but the benefits dissipate if practice is discontinued. Certain practitioners can increase blood flow to the body periphery, thereby raising the temperature of fingers and toes. Tibetan Tumo masters who specialize in this are reported to demonstrate their mastery by meditating seminaked in the snows of the Tibetan winter.

Blood chemistry may also shift. Hormone levels may be modified, lactate levels—sometimes regarded as a measure of relaxation—may fall, and cholesterol may be reduced.

The most common measure of brain activity during meditation has been the EEG, which provides a measure of cerebral electrical activity that is valuable but gross—comparable to measuring activity in Chicago by placing a dozen microphones around it. While it remains unclear whether there are patterns unique to meditation, intriguing findings have emerged.

With most meditative practices the EEG slows and more synchronous alpha waves (8–13 cycles per second) increase in amount and amplitude. In more advanced practitioners even greater slowing may occur and theta (4–7 cycles) patterns may appear. These findings are consistent with deep relaxation. Not only do the brain waves slow but they may also show increasing synchronization or coherence between different cortical areas. Some TM researchers suggest that this provides a basis for enhanced creativity and psychological growth. However, it is always difficult in EEG research to extrapolate from brain waves to specific states of mind and it is usefully humbling to realize that greater coherence can also occur in epilepsy and schizophrenia.

It is increasingly recognized that the left and right cerebral hemispheres have distinct, though overlapping, functions. Because meditation may reduce left hemisphere functions such as verbal analysis, meditation might involve either a reduction of left hemisphere activity and/or an activation of the right hemisphere. There is preliminary evidence of some enhanced right hemisphere skills in meditators such as the ability to remember and discriminate musical tones. However, EEG studies suggest that while there may be relative left hemisphere deactivation during the initial few minutes of a sitting, thereafter both hemispheres seem to be affected equally.

Yogis and Zen practitioners may respond differently to sensory stimulation, in ways consistent with their respective methods and goals of practice. In early studies that deserve repetition, yogis, whose practice involves internal focus and withdrawal of attention from the senses, showed little EEG response to repeated noises. However, Zen monks whose practice involves open receptivity to all stimuli showed continued EEG responsiveness to a repeated sound, rather than habituating to it as nonmeditators would. Although other studies have found less clear-cut differences, these findings remain intriguing since the electrophysiological data are consistent with both the different goals and experiences of yogic and Zen practitioners.

Therapeutic Effects

Many effects of meditation seem beneficial and research suggests that it can be therapeutic for various psychological and psychosomatic disorders. Of course, as with other therapies, psychological distress can occur during meditation as previously repressed psychological traumas and blocks are experienced. Responsive psychological disorders include anxiety, phobias, post-traumatic stress, muscle tension, insomnia and mild depression. Regular long-term meditation seems to reduce both legal and illegal drug use and to help prisoners by reducing anxiety, aggression and recidivism.

Psychosomatic benefits may include reduction in blood pressure, cholesterol and the severity of asthma, migraine and chronic pain.

These therapeutic effects may reflect enhanced general psy-

118

chological and physical health. In fact TM meditators use less than normal amounts of psychiatric and medical care and meditators in their mid-50s measured twelve years younger than controls on scales of physical aging. Of course, how much of this superior general health is actually due to meditation and how much to associated factors such as prior good health and a healthy lifestyle is unclear. . . .

How Meditation May Work

Exactly how meditation produces its many effects remains unclear. Many mechanisms have been suggested. Possible physiological processes include lowered arousal and increased hemispheric synchronization. Possible psychological mechanisms include relaxation, desensitization, dehypnosis, and development of self-control skills, insight and self-understanding. Perhaps the most encompassing exploration is the classic one: namely that meditation fosters psychological development.

While much has been learned experimentally about meditation, research is still in its early stages. As yet, relatively little can be said about the relationships between the traditional goals of meditation and experimental measures. More attention has been given to heart rate than heart opening. Future research will need to pay more attention to advanced practitioners and their transpersonal goals such as enhanced concentration, ethics, love, compassion, generosity, wisdom and service. The vision of a mutually enriching bridge between meditation and science remains only partly realized, but it also remains worth seeking.

"Meditation may bring about a variety of undesirable changes—physical, mental, and emotional."

Meditation Can Be Harmful

Nathaniel Mead

In the following viewpoint, Nathaniel Mead raises questions about the safety and efficacy of meditation. Mead, a health writer and frequent contributor to the bimonthly magazine *Natural Health*, suggests that meditation may actually cause physical and mental problems for some people who use it simply to reduce stress and promote health and well-being.

As you read, consider the following questions:

1. According to Mead, why is meditation sometimes "medically ill-advised"?
2. According to the author, how can an activity most people use to calm nerves increase anxiety?

Nathaniel Mead, "Why Meditation May Not Reduce Stress," *Natural Health*, November/December 1993. Reprinted with permission. For a trial issue of *Natural Health*, call 1-800-526-8440.

Frank Jones sits cross-legged on a mat, his eyes closed, arms and shoulders limp. Slowly, he tunes in to each part of his body, from head to toe, noting the slightest change or sensation. No matter what he detects—pain, tension, discomfort—he simply lets it enter his awareness, then moves on. Occasionally, he turns his attention to the slow, rhythmic flow of his breath, which soon begins to resemble the pattern of restful sleep.

This particular technique, known to many as mindfulness, is said to be the perfect antidote to the hectic lives of workaholics like Frank, whose idea of fun consists of speed-reading the business sections of several newspapers on his half-hour lunch break.

Within minutes of beginning today's sitting session, however, Frank's feeling of peace is short-lived. His face turns from serene to troubled. His heartbeat begins to race, and tightness grips his upper back muscles. The painful knots of muscle tension inch from his back and neck upward, producing a constricting sensation, as if a steel band had formed around his head. Ten minutes later, now fidgety and perspiring, he ends the session with a gasp of relief.

Meditation is often presented as a benign way to relieve stress and improve overall health, but some research points to situations in which the practice may be upsetting, inappropriate, or even medically ill-advised. Indeed, under certain conditions, meditation may bring about a variety of undesirable changes— physical, mental, and emotional. Frank's experience, referred to by meditation researchers as "relaxation-induced panic," is but one of several possible side effects of meditating.

When meditation first became popular with Americans in the 1960s, its primary purpose was to deepen personal awareness and promote spiritual growth. Since that time, however, meditation has increasingly been used as a stress-reduction technique and as a way to bolster the body's healing potential. One source of meditation problems comes from the attempt to turn a powerful psychological technique into a simple physical therapy. When a meditator is led to expect stress reduction and instead comes face to face with his true self, the result can be anything but relaxing.

Among the positive effects most often associated with meditation is progressive, physical and mental relaxation. But the effect can backfire. Psychiatrist and longtime meditation researcher Arnold A. Lazarus reported in a 1990 issue of *Psychotherapy* that such relaxation effects can paradoxically lead to "increases in tension" and "relaxation-induced anxiety and panic." Previously, Lazarus had reported a number of incidents where learning Transcendental Meditation, a consciousness-raising technique from India, seemed to promote certain psychiatric problems. Several of his patients said that TM increased their feelings of depression, and some said that the practice tended to heighten their already existent anxieties and restlessness. One of his female patients made a suicide attempt following a weekend training course in the technique. In another case, a schizophrenic breakdown was apparently triggered by TM.

Similar problems have been reported by psychologist Leon Otis of the Stanford Research Institute in Menlo Park, California. Otis tells of five subjects who, after commencing meditation, suffered from serious psychosomatic symptoms that had previously been under control. These included a bleeding ulcer (under control for the past five years), a recurrence of depression requiring medication, and for one subject, extreme agitation that resulted in termination of employment. . . .

Routine Difficulties

Many meditation instructors would agree that the difficulties encountered by these meditators are routine. The Buddhist tradition speaks directly about the problems, or "hindrances," encountered by those on the spiritual path. In contrast, westernized forms of meditation are expected to reduce problems and anxiety through muscle relaxation and lowering of blood pressure. Often associated with stress-management approaches like biofeedback and guided imagery, meditation is typically perceived as a relaxation technique that helps people "cope" in the high-pressure arena of modern life. In such instances, meditation is not normally practiced to resolve emotional conflicts or to produce a spiritual awakening, though it may inadvertently lead to this.

Mark Epstein, a New York–based psychiatrist with a long-standing interest in Buddhist meditation, has written extensively on the subject and frequently does therapy with people who meditate. Epstein says, "By no means do people automatically get relaxed when they start to meditate. Though meditation can relax the body, it's really about investigating what's happening in the mind and in the body, at any given moment. All kinds of peculiar, anxiety-making things can happen in the mind or body at any time. When people start meditating, they can get anxious because of what they uncover by looking within."

The list of side effects compiled by meditation teachers and researchers is remarkably long. These include momentary discomforts such as headaches, sore throats, cramped muscles, and tingling or stinging sensations in some parts of the body. Some people have reported feeling unaccountably heavy, while others experience weightlessness or floating sensations. One person may "see" all kinds of fascinating images, while others may have the intense impression that they can smell certain scents or taste certain flavors. Some report sudden outbursts of laughter or crying, or both. Involuntary sighing, as well as sweating, trembling, or shivering, are also common.

"*Prayer of surrender plays an important role in healing.*"

Prayer Can Heal

Rosemary Ellen Guiley

In the following viewpoint, Rosemary Ellen Guiley maintains that prayer is an important element in spiritual and physical healing. She recounts several incidents in which people suffering terminal illness or an irreversible condition were cured of their affliction through prayer. According to Guiley, prayer releases a tremendous energy that can heal spiritual or physical distress. Guiley is the author of *The Miracle of Prayer: True Stories of Blessed Healing*.

As you read, consider the following questions:

1. What are three of the anecdotes that Guiley relates to illustrate the efficacy of prayer in reversing illness?
2. According to the author, what are the different kinds of prayer and how are they used?
3. What is the "key secret" to successful prayer, according to William "Cherry" Parker, cited by Guiley?

Excerpted from Rosemary Ellen Guiley, "The New Millennium," *Fate*, May 1995. Reprinted with permission.

Ann Marie Davis, a Unity minister in Clinton, Iowa, was 30 years old when she lay dying in a Minnesota hospital, her body ravaged by cancer and Legionnaires' disease. The cancer—her fourth recurrence since childhood—was serious, but it was the Legionnaires' disease that was threatening to kill her. Her lungs had turned brittle. Lung tissue is normally rubbery, and, according to doctors, when it turns brittle, it cannot be restored. When lungs turn brittle, you cannot breathe without a respirator. Ann Marie was not expected to live through the night and doctors advised her family to prepare for her death.

The next morning, Ann Marie had recovered, and her cancer was gone. The doctors couldn't explain the turnaround.

What took place during the night to repair a body that doctors said was irrevocably damaged? The change was a miracle, and miracles forever remain a mystery. What Ann Marie did was surrender herself to God through prayer.

Today Ann Marie is 45, and she is so bright and vibrant it is difficult to think that she was ever seriously ill.

Research on Prayer

Ann Marie was one of many remarkable, inspiring people I've met while I've been researching the power of prayer, especially in healing. In England, I met Dr. Kai Kermani, a physician who suffers from retinitis pigmentosa, a progressive, irreversible blindness. Using deep meditation and prayer, Kai reversed the disease and restored partial vision. He now works as a spiritual healer. In Scotland, I met Guy Riggs, who turned to prayer while he lay on a rocky beach with a broken back from a fall, hoping to be rescued before the tide came in and drowned him.

Near Kansas City, at Unity headquarters, I met Jim Rosemergy, who used prayer to restore partial sight to an eye that had lost vision after a blood vessel burst. And I met Maurice Williams, whose prayers helped him through life-threatening kidney failure. I met others who had prayed during fires, tornadoes, and hurricanes and were spared damage and injury. People whose prayers helped them recover from substance and physical abuse. People who experienced spiritual openings after prayer. The literature on prayer, plus lab studies and dramatic testimonies, speaks to the tremendous power released in the act of praying.

The Power of Prayer

For much of my life, I was a perfunctory pray-er. Like many people, I learned to pray in childhood, at home and in church. But prayer seemed dry and remote. I read about its power, but I could not feel that power myself.

As an adult, I became interested in meditation, visualization, and affirmation, and began doing those daily. These are related to prayer; they can even be considered forms of prayer. They seek to put consciousness on a higher level and to effect change.

In the mid-1980s, I became aware of the angelic realm, and I also became interested in spiritual healing. These returned me to traditional prayer, which I blended into my spiritual practices. Now I felt the power of prayer—how it connects us to the divine, how it helps us help ourselves and others. I've not had any life-threatening situations, but I've had many instances in which I've felt the power of prayer work in my life.

Prayer is a complex subject that acts rather like quicksilver. No matter how we try to define it and contain it, its true shape is elusive.

Communing with God

William James once noted that prayer "is the very soul and essence of religion." Essentially, prayer is an act of communing with God, or the divine, or the supernatural, or the universal mind—pick your term depending on your spiritual or religious outlook. Prayer has existed in numerous forms since the human race became conscious. It is fundamental to all religions.

Yet prayer thrives outside organized religion. It is the essential link that helps us bridge two worlds—our mundane world and a transcendent reality in which we see all things as possible.

The simplest and most common form of prayer is the petition, in which we ask for something for ourselves. The word *prayer* itself means to petition, coming from the Latin term *precarius*, which means "obtained by begging." Most of us make petitionary prayers on an almost daily basis whenever we want something to go right, or when we want something to change. The question of who to petition is a big one. Depending on religion and cultural background, we petition God, the goddess, the divine, saints, angels, the ancestral dead, hosts of spirits, or even forces of nature.

Another common form of prayer is the intercession, in which we ask for help for another person. Petition and intercession are instrumental in healing.

Healing Prayers

Other kinds of prayer are thanksgiving, adoration, confession, lamentation, meditation, contemplation, and surrender. Meditation and contemplation are mystical in nature. These kinds of prayers are instrumental in healing, especially healing into wholeness—the kind of healing that takes place on the level of the soul and in the inner chambers of the heart. Plato once observed that "if the head and the body are to be well, you must begin by curing the soul; that is the first thing . . . the great er-

125

ror of our day in the treatment of the human body (is) that physicians separate the soul from the body."

Prayer of surrender plays an important role in healing. Rather than ask for specifics, the prayer of surrender turns the resolution over to divine will. It asks nothing, and accepts whatever the outcome is. Many people who pray regularly—and who have had stunning experiences with other kinds of prayer—find that ultimately, the best, most effective prayer is one of surrender.

Prayer of surrender is what Ann Marie Davis did. I asked her how she prays now. "There's no one way to pray," she says. "I pray more affirmative prayers now [than petitionary]. I also pray to surrender. Every time I surrender, the problem is taken care of. Another way I pray is what we in Unity call sitting in silence (meditation), in which we let go of thought. But surrender and trust—that's the quickest way to heal. And don't have attachment to the outcome—know that you can accept whatever the outcome is."

Intercessory Prayer

There are a large number of controlled laboratory experiments showing that intercessory prayer has a significant effect in a host of biological organisms. . . .

I regard this information collectively as one of the best-kept secrets in medical science. Physicians, for the most part, have never heard of it. If taken seriously, this information could revolutionize our understanding of the nature of consciousness, the relationship between mind and brain, and the actual dynamics of healing.

Larry Dossey, *Resurgence*, November/December 1993.

As Ann Marie mentioned, there is no one right way to pray. Prayer is unique to each person, even when standard prayers such as the Lord's Prayer are used. Sometimes it is appropriate to ask for help for ourselves, sometimes for others. Sometimes it is better to surrender.

People often ask why some prayers seem to be unanswered. Why do some people pray for healings that don't come? Such questions are hard to answer. Every situation involving prayer is complex, with many subtle factors at work. Prayer involves more than a collection of words, thoughts, and intents. We may be undergoing certain trials in order to learn lessons on a soul level. If we pray for deliverance or relief, we may not get quite what we expect.

The apostle James said prayers that seem to be unanswered mean that "ye ask amiss"; in other words, one does not ask for what is right, or with sufficient faith. Charles Fillmore, the co-founder of Unity, said that faith acts like electricity that speeds the answers to prayers. If no answer is forthcoming, that means a lack of "proper mental adjustment of the mind" on the part of the pray-er.

No answer can also be an answer, however; thus, prayers are always answered. Sometimes the answer is not the one we want to hear. Sometimes the answer is "no" to what we ask.

"Prayer is not like turning on the oven," observes Daniel J. Benor, M.D., one of the leading researchers in complementary medicine. "We pray because we are not in control. Maybe we want a quick fix—we want God to solve our problem when we need to be doing the work ourselves.

"The reason for illness may be beyond our immediate compre-hension. We may have lessons to learn through the illness or other problems. Part of our lesson may be with people who are close to us. Maybe we have not learned to ask for help from those around us. Part of healing may be releasing old hurts."

Some years ago, researcher William "Cherry" Parker conducted a study of prayer and came up with a key secret to successful prayer: total honesty. Be completely honest with yourself and with God concerning your motives and what you are asking for.

The healer Ambrose Worrall observed that every thought is a prayer. "In healing, the essence of the thought may achieve in an instant where a thousand verbalized entreaties fail," Worrall wrote in *The Gift of Healing*. "This is not because no one is lis-tening, but because we, perhaps, ask amiss, because we are dealing not with whim but with universal law. . . . Whether or not we go to church regularly, we still lead prayerful lives, though we may not know it."

"Prayers for healing continue, some effectively utilizing known psychosomatic processes, . . . as well as those disappointing cases where God seems to have said 'no.'"

Prayer May Not Be Able to Heal

William B. Lindley

In the following viewpoint, William B. Lindley maintains that while in some instances prayer may produce a placebo effect (a well-documented medical phenomenon in which the body heals because the mind believes a cure is working), he is skeptical about claims that prayer can actually heal illness or injury. Lindley contends that there is little evidence of prayer's efficacy and no scientific way of proving that prayer can help heal. Lindley is the associate editor of *Truth Seeker*, an independent journal of opinion.

As you read, consider the following questions:

1. Why does the author conclude that prayers for football games are more effective than prayers to cure illness?
2. What experiments have been done in an attempt to prove that prayer can effect a certain outcome, according to Lindley?

William B. Lindley, "Prayer and Healing," *Truth Seeker*, vol. 122, no. 2, 1995. Reprinted with permission.

I was raised in Christian Science. That gives me somewhat of an inside perspective on prayer and healing. However, the Christian Science experience is far from typical. The "Scientific Statement of Being" begins: "There is no life, truth, intelligence nor substance in matter." Most Christians who offer prayers of petition for the healing of an illness believe that their bodies are real and the illness is real, but they want supernatural intervention, the sort of thing Jesus is reported to have done in the gospels. Christian Science, interpreting Jesus' work quite differently insists that reality lies elsewhere. The analogue to prayer is "knowing the truth." Christian Science insists that miracles are not "supernatural, but divinely natural."

As I grew up and matter made more sense to me, I drifted away from Christian Science. Then I began hearing about natural, nonmiraculous analogues to what I had been taught: psychosomatic diseases and cures, the placebo effect, and, more recently, the neurochemical connections between mood and the immune system. These, along with "spontaneous remission" of cancers, were attempts to explain "miracles" without invoking the supernatural or the paranormal. (Note that "spontaneous" (natural), and "God did it" (supernatural), are "explanations" that explain nothing. There's no "how.") Believers in miracles—evangelicals, Christian Scientists, miscellaneous New Agers, and so forth—continue as before.

Prayer and Healing

Healing Words by Larry Dossey, M.D., is a book devoted to prayer and healing, and its author believes firmly that prayer (communication with "the Absolute") brings about beneficial effects that are real and substantial and supernatural or paranormal in character. However, when he raises the question, "What is prayer?", the answer is so far-ranging that all sorts of things that would not ordinarily be considered prayer are included. He rejects the Christian concept of prayer! Of course he doesn't use such strong language as "reject," preferring slippery words like "redefine," "tentative" and "reevaluate." He has a chart contrasting the "traditional Western model" with the "modern" model of prayer. Probably over 95% of the prayers for healing that are made in the United States would be of the "old" model, which Dossey considers obsolete. Interestingly enough, Christian Science prayer would fall under the 5% that he would approve of.

Even though Dossey seems to think little of traditional prayer, his citations of many experiments that allegedly demonstrate the efficacy of prayer do not indicate whether the style of prayer was traditional or otherwise. (He clearly expresses his opinion that all kinds work, some better than others.) The experiments are broken down into various categories of what was

129

prayed over—barley seeds(!), mice, people, etc.—but not into categories of what kind of prayer was made.

Sometimes Dossey seems to be unaware of the implications of what he says. For example, he quotes psychologist Lawrence LeShan to the effect that healing through prayer is effective in perhaps 15 to 20% of cases and that nobody can tell in advance which cases will have happy outcomes. Somewhat disheartened by this, Dossey goes on to claim that prayer works anyway. Then he mentions the "bizarre," "perverted" use of prayer by high school football teams in Texas, where, of course, they offer up highly unsportsmanlike prayers for victory. Such prayers obviously "work" 50% of the time. (We might cut this to 48% or so for tie games.) Thus one can conclude that prayer for victory in football is three times as efficacious as prayer for healing!

The Problems of Prayer

Dossey wisely reminds us that if all prayers for healing led to success, population growth would be even more catastrophic than it is; 100% success rates for other kinds of prayer could have other horrible long-term effects. (Billy Graham put it a little differently: "God answers all prayers; sometimes the answer is 'no.'") However, once this is admitted—and note that it flatly contradicts Jesus' promise in Matthew 7:7,8: "Ask, and it will be given you; search, and you will find; knock, and the door will be opened for you. For everyone who asks receives, and everyone who searches finds, and for everyone who knocks, the door will be opened"—the result is indistinguishable from that of no prayer at all.

Healing Cults

Science is under attack from many quarters these days, and healing cults are yet another part of that attack. Cults appeal to those of a mystical mind-set who want the world and their bodies to be more responsive to their hopes than the scientific evidence permits us to believe.

Arnold S. Relman, *Wall Street Journal*, July 12, 1995.

Another problem is the intent of the person praying. Others who have faced the incoherent attempts to define prayer have said that the essence of prayer, whether there be a Supreme Being or not, is that the person praying must intend, or want, or be praying for, a particular happy ending to the current crisis. However, Dossey rejects the concept of intent. He states: "For reasons I shall discuss later, never once did I pray for specific outcomes—for cancers to go away, for heart attacks to be healed, for diabetes to vanish." He reports on an interesting group, Spindrift, that provides many "proofs" that prayer works. This group had a number of Christian Scientists in it. (One was a Christian Science practitioner whose "license" was revoked after The First Church of Christ, Scientist found out what he was up to.) Spindrift took up the question of directed vs. undirected prayer, and found that the undirected prayer worked somewhat better. Most of the other experiments by other groups, for example, with barley seeds, were directed—the intent to have the seeds flourish was in the minds of the people who prayed over them.

Prayer Experiments

Let's take a closer look at those experiments. There is a long list of them. The compiler is Daniel J. Benor, M.D. He published his survey in the journal *Complementary Medical Research* in 1990. The activity is called "spiritual healing," and this is defined as "the intentional influence of one or more people upon another living system without utilizing known physical means of intervention." (Note how this differs from the Spindrift effort cited above and from Dossey's preference for nondirected prayer.) Of 131 trials, five involved water, with three showing "significant results," but what was being prayed for in the water cases is not mentioned. There were ten trials of "enzymes," including trypsin, dopamine, and noradrenaline. (Are these enzymes? I think not.) There were seven trials on fungi and yeasts, with some prayers being for, some against, the prosperous growth of the culture. Similarly for the ten trials on bacteria, mainly E. coli and salmonella. Cells in vitro (tube or glass dish) were prayed over, including four trials on snail pacemaker cells. There were 19 trials on plants and seeds, including five on the above-mentioned barley seeds. Three of these involved different kinds of person praying: one with neurotic depression, one with psychotic depression, and one with a green thumb. As you might guess, the last showed the strongest beneficial effect. Other plants and seeds prayed over include: rye grass, wheat seeds, radish seeds, mung beans, potatoes and corn. The prayer trials on animals include 14 on anesthetized mice, with a variety of experimental conditions and effects sought. Humans were also prayed over for a total of 38 of the 131 trials. Some of the conditions prayed over are obviously psychosomatic, some less so. Clearly there is an enthusiastic "spiritual healing research" community doing many things we wouldn't ordinarily think of.

Something I was unable to find in all this is any breakdown by religion of the person praying. Christians would consider it vital to ask whether the words "In Jesus' name we pray, amen" were spoken. If they weren't, the Christians would be extremely skeptical of the efficacy of the prayers. If they were confronted by overwhelming evidence that a non-Christian prayer was highly effective, they would suspect Satanism and look for evidence of it. Similarly perhaps for Muslims. Catholics might accept evidence of efficacy of prayers invoking the Trinity while being skeptical of those with Protestant prayer tags. Regrettably, the 131 trials provide us with no information along these lines.

Another missing factor that I regret is a detailed skeptical review of the experimental methodology of some of the more impressive trials. The Committee for the Scientific Investigation of Claims of the Paranormal seems to be silent in this area. While they have offered some criticism of Therapeutic Touch, they seem to be silent on the question of religious prayer healing, except in "revivals," where some noteworthy frauds have been exposed. This is part of a pattern. Most of the subjects discussed in the *Skeptical Inquirer* are New Age phenomena, such as crop circles, UFOs, pyramid power, astrology, and so on. CSICOP seems to be leaving Christianity alone, at least for the time being. Dossey's book cries for skeptical attention. As in the other cases, such attention would have to be very painstaking, time-consuming, and expensive.

Meanwhile, prayers for healing continue, some effectively utilizing known psychosomatic processes, others producing remarkable placebo effects (the same thing, except that we don't know what's happening), and many more where supernatural claims are made, as well as those disappointing cases where God seems to have said "no."

Periodical Bibliography

The following articles have been selected to supplement the diverse views presented in this chapter. Addresses are provided for periodicals not indexed in the *Readers' Guide to Periodical Literature*, the *Alternative Press Index*, or the *Social Sciences Index*.

Elaine Appleton	"To Bee or Not to Bee?" *New Age Journal*, February 1995. Available from 42 Pleasant St., Watertown, MA 02172.
At the Crossroads	"Chalk One Up for Homeopathy," no. 6, 1995. Available from PO Box 112, St. Paul, AR 72760.
Loyd Auerbach	"Psychic Frontiers," *Fate*, August 1994. Available from Llewellyn Worldwide, 84 S. Wabasha, St. Paul, MN 55107.
Karen Baar	"The Real Options in Healthcare," *Natural Health*, November/December 1994. Available from 17 Station St., Brookline Village, MA 02147.
Stephen Barrett	"Questionable Cancer Therapies," *Priorities*, vol. 7, no. 2, 1995. Available from 1995 Broadway, 2nd Fl., New York, NY 10023-5860.
Chip Brown	"The Experiments of Dr. Oz," *New York Times Magazine*, July 30, 1995.
Vern L. Bullough and Bonnie Bullough	"Therapeutic Touch: Why Do Nurses Believe?" *Skeptical Inquirer*, vol. 17, no. 2, Winter 1993. Available from 3025 Palo Alto Dr. NE, Albuquerque, NM 87111.
Jean Callahan	"Studying the Alternatives," *New Age Journal*, January/February 1995.
Geoffrey Cowley et al.	"Going Mainstream," *Newsweek*, June 26, 1995.
Larry Dossey	"Science and Healing," *Resurgence*, November/December 1993. Available from Ford House, Hartland, Bideford, Devon, EX39 6EE, UK.
Henry Dreher	"Proven Mind/Body Medicine," *Natural Health*, May/June 1993.
David M. Eisenberg et al.	"Unconventional Medicine in the United States," *New England Journal of Medicine*, vol. 328, no. 4, January 28, 1993. Available from 10 Shattuck St., Boston, MA 02115-6094.

Tiffany Field	"Massage Therapy for Infants and Children," *Developmental and Behavioral Pediatrics*, vol. 16, no. 2, April 1995. Available from Plenum Publishing, 233 Spring St., New York, NY 10013.
Adriane Fugh-Berman	"The Case for 'Natural' Medicine," *Nation*, September 6–13, 1993.
Rosemary Ellen Guiley	"The New Millennium," *Fate*, September 1995.
J. Allan Hobson	"Sleep and the Immune System," *Truth Seeker*, vol. 122, no. 2, 1995. Available from 16935 W. Bernardo Dr., Suite 103, San Diego, CA 92127.
Andrea Honebrink	"Meditation: Hazardous to Your Health?" *Utne Reader*, March/April 1994.
Marilynn Larkin	"NIH's Office of Alternative Medicine: A Wise Use of Our Tax Dollars?" *Priorities*, vol. 6, no. 4, 1994.
Michael Lerner	"Hedging the Bet Against Cancer," *New York Times Magazine*, October 2, 1994.
Kathleen Meister	"Beyond the Beef About Beef," *Priorities*, Spring 1993.
Steve Salerno	"Pain: It Doesn't Have to Hurt," *American Legion*, vol. 138, no. 6, June 1995. Available from 5561 W. 74th St., Indianapolis, IN 46268.
Anastasia Toufexis	"Dr. Jacobs' Alternative Mission," *Time*, March 1, 1993.

Is the Health Care Industry Effective?

*H*ealth
*F*and
itness

Chapter Preface

As medical costs have escalated in recent years, a new approach to providing health care has emerged: managed care. Managed care is a system in which insurance providers control costs by closely monitoring and supervising the care that is provided to patients. Health maintenance organizations (HMOs) are the most common—and perhaps the most controversial—type of managed care system.

Members of HMOs pay a fixed monthly fee, which is usually quite low, in return for basic health care treatment at a low cost. HMO advocates contend that the organizations provide high-quality health care while containing costs. According to Alain C. Enthoven, a Stanford management professor, and Richard Kronick, a senior health policy adviser in the Clinton administration, HMOs simultaneously ensure good care and low cost by "selecting doctors carefully for quality and economy, monitoring their performance and making sure their knowledge is up to date." Enthoven, Kronick, and others maintain that the recent rapid growth in HMO membership is evidence that the organizations provide good care. "Without quality care," argues Westcott W. Price III, the CEO of FHP International Corp., "there is no way HMO membership would have grown so dramatically."

Others contend that HMOs, in their zeal to control costs, often provide substandard or insufficient care to their members. Critics charge that HMO doctors are given financial incentives to limit the number of tests and treatments they offer to their patients and that, consequently, patients are often denied needed services. In addition, according to critics, HMO doctors are prevented in various ways from ordering outside tests and referring patients to specialists, which in turn results in patients' receiving inaccurate diagnoses and inadequate treatments. According to Ellyn E. Spragins of *Newsweek* magazine, "If you're sick and require expensive tests or consultations with specialists, there's mounting evidence that your HMO might delay (or deny outright) crucial care."

Observing the growth of HMOs, Nancy J. Perry, a senior editor for *Money* magazine, writes, "It's dawning on millions of Americans that HMOs loom large in their immediate futures." Whether the presence of HMOs will prove harmful or beneficial is one of the issues discussed in the following chapter.

"The public and primary health care infrastructure . . . has been dismantled and abandoned."

America's Health Care System Is in Crisis

Nancy F. McKenzie

In the following viewpoint, Nancy F. McKenzie argues that due to cuts in public health programs and a decline in the number of doctors willing to treat poor patients, the health care needs of many Americans—especially minorities and the poor—are not being adequately met. McKenzie contends that the current health care system is centered on creating profit rather than on providing for the social good, resulting in a decline in the quality of health care nationwide. McKenzie is the editor of *Beyond Crisis: Confronting Health Care in the U.S.*

As you read, consider the following questions:

1. What safety net programs were cut between 1980 and 1992, according to McKenzie? By how much does she say they were cut?
2. According to the author, what epidemics have emerged as a result of a lack of emphasis on prevention?
3. What have "medicine" and "health care" become metaphors for, in McKenzie's opinion?

Nancy F. McKenzie, "The Real Health Care Crisis," *Nation*, February 28, 1994. Reprinted with permission from *The Nation* magazine; © The Nation Company, L.P.

Lately, as the debate over health care reform has grown more heated, more scrambled and more overloaded by competing lobbies, a new approach has surfaced offering a respite to those overwhelmed by the mind-numbing details: Relax, there is no health care crisis. You can hear it from Clinton friend and foe alike. "Our country has health care problems, but no health care crisis," growled Senator Bob Dole in his televised response to the President's 1994 State of the Union Message. Days earlier, Democratic Senator Pat Moynihan said pretty much the same on *Meet the Press*. What nonsense!

In fact, health care in America is beyond crisis. We are currently suffering the effects of the skewed health financing policies of the past thirty years. The Reagan/Bush era saw the economic rout of everyone but the very rich, and in health care the dismantling of public programs, preventive care and basic physician education and training, as well as the failure to oversee private insurers. Cuts in safety-net programs between 1980 and 1992 were substantial: 23 percent in maternal health services, 28 percent in preventive health services, 40 percent in community clinics (after adjusting for the health care inflation rate), 63 percent in community development and housing assistance.

Exclusion of the Poor

Today, only a small portion of doctors choose to provide primary care—family practice services, internal medicine, obstetrics/gynecology—and only a small percentage of those will treat poor patients. Public entitlements are so restrictive in their coverage and meager in their payments to physicians that many who do provide basic care are opting out of Medicaid altogether as well as parts of the Medicare program. The institutional exclusion of the sick poor also occurs in the private arena. A 1990 study in New York City found a total of just twenty-eight primary-care physicians for 1.6 million people in the city's nine lowest income communities. In New York State, only 15 percent of physicians regularly see Medicaid patients. And in major cities across the nation, 50 percent of all admissions to public hospitals are through the emergency room because so many individuals lack physicians. The result:

• The maternal mortality rate of women of color is three times that of white women. One-half to one-third of these deaths are unnecessary and could easily be avoided using preventive measures, given that they are primarily attributable to lack of prenatal care.

• Because they come so late to treatment, only 22 percent of women diagnosed with breast cancer at New York City's Harlem Hospital live five years, compared with 76 percent of white women and 64 percent of black women nationwide.

• A child in Chile or Malaysia is more likely to celebrate his first birthday than a black baby born in the Mississippi Delta.
• Black men in central Harlem are less likely to reach age 65 than men in Bangladesh.
• Estimates of HIV infection among homeless individuals go as high as 40 percent.
• After controlling for differences in age, sex, race and specific disease, the uninsured are as much as three times more likely to die during a hospital stay than the insured.

The Poor and Minorities Are Underserved

There are currently 40 million Americans in 2,437 urban and rural areas who do not have access to adequate primary-care medicine. Nearly 11,000 primary-care doctors are needed to help these communities reach the government's target rate of 1 doctor for every 2,000 residents. While this problem crosses racial and income lines in rural settings, it is most prevalent in areas with heavy concentrations of low-income and minority populations. A study co-authored by David Kindig of the University of Wisconsin at Madison School of Medicine found that all predominantly African-American and Hispanic rural counties in the United States have physician-population ratios lower than both the national average and the average of all nonurban counties. Kindig's research indicates that a 10 percent increase in a rural county's black population lowers the number of doctors by 1.9 per 100,000 people. Similarly, a decrease of $1,000 in per capita income is associated with a decline of 4.4 doctors per 100,000 people.

The same pattern holds true in urban areas. Doctors in cities tend to cluster in wealthier areas—where residents are more likely to have private insurance—and avoid neighborhoods with large numbers of low-income people. Says Ina Labiner, executive director of the Community Health Care Association of New York State: "There are more than enough doctors in [New York City], but they are on Park Avenue, not in Harlem, not in the South Bronx, not in Bedford-Stuyvesant."

Sara Collins, *U.S. News & World Report*, September 20, 1993.

In the United States over the past twenty years, health care increasingly has been redefined to mean the provision of medical services alone. Broader threats to health, such as lead poisoning, stress and lack of housing, as well as rehabilitative strategies and long-term care, have all dropped out of health discourse. The predictable result is that the system is now besieged by public health crises it is unequipped to handle. For twelve years [as of 1994] we have had an AIDS epidemic that, by international standards, is unnecessarily vast. In 1988 there was a syphilis scare. In 1989–90 there was a measles epidemic due to a national shrinking of childhood immunization programs. Now it is tuberculosis.

The Latest Disaster

Since 1984, the United States has been ravaged by a tuberculosis epidemic of staggering proportions, largely among individuals between the ages of 25 and 44. Despite the preventability and curability of TB, cases in New York City, for example, have doubled since 1985, to 52 per 100,000 in 1992 (the national incidence was 10.5 cases per 100,000). New York City's black and Latino communities have five times the national average, and comprise 80 percent of cases in the state. Currently, 19 percent of TB cases in the city are multiple-drug resistant because of inconsistent treatment and individuals' lack of connection to health facilities. As a result, public health officials here and abroad are worried that America has created a new and essentially untreatable TB strain.

The response to the current TB epidemic reveals not only the inadequacy of the health care system but the limitations of the current debate on health care reform. The re-emergence and flourishing of this nineteenth-century disease is only the latest wave of health disasters to batter a population increasingly lacking in housing, employment and public and primary health care; that is, more and more people lack the basic human services essential for a community's well-being. The current debate ignores the fact that the public and primary health care infrastructure, which could be expected to treat TB patients, has been dismantled and abandoned, or increasingly replaced by managed-care cost containment programs. . . .

Health Care as Commodity

The problem is that there is no rational structure of health care in the United States, just a marketplace for the buying and selling of life and death. Judging from the narrowness of the current debate, most people seem to have accepted a system that is wholly profit based; in which the pieces of health care they receive—or don't receive—are commodities like all others in a highly developed global economy; in which arguments about decency, justice and responsibility are inappropriate. Hence the focus on controlling costs rather than improving lives. Like a phantom limb, discussion of health care as a social good kicks in at moments but, by and large, it has become an amputated discourse.

Today, most middle-income Americans apparently expect a health care system that responds to public needs about as much as we expect a good public transportation system. Yet individuals also know that something larger, more awful is happening to us: "Medicine" or "health care" is becoming a metaphor for neglect, for what might be monstrous about American life devoid of a belief in the common good. Our caretakers have receded behind institutions with darker, more meanspirited goals. Commodification is one thing; the commodification of medicine is quite another.

Everyone feels the continental shift when the doctor becomes the purveyor, when medicine becomes the corporation and M.B.A.s the moral arbiters. And this does not happen overnight, or directly. . . . The American health care system is made up of institutions and entire agencies that function as business managers, executing the financial directives of those providers or regulators. If the institutions in America had a strong health agenda, individual practitioners would not be entrepreneurs. Opportunism and the exploitation of individuals originate within institutions and are hidden by the technical jargon of advanced education. When this happens, as it has in the management mentality that has infected all areas of American life, it is a loss. In health care it is a mortal danger.

The HIV epidemic has taught Americans that getting a catastrophic disease can change one's class status. Poverty begets disease, and disease begets poverty. Both serve as sources of stigmatization within and exclusion from a national health system wholly tuned to profit. The dominant rhetoric of cost containment in health care has so perverted discourse, it is almost impossible to articulate the loss in reasonableness, humaneness, decency.

There are signs of resistance. The very breakdown of social obligation in our institutions has fostered a new set of "informal" relations of obligation. Whether it is between ACT UP [AIDS Coalition to Unleash Power] and the Food and Drug Administration, among providers of health care in shelters or in migrant worker camps, among citizens in cities working on the front line against the invisibility of whole communities, a new health activism across race and class lines is calling for a new shape to the health and social policies of the United States. As the system approaches chaos, individuals—many of them with nothing left to lose—gain sight of their own power to help and be helped. If this new activism among the coalitions representing those at multiple jeopardy becomes a true political movement, it could well gain momentum as the civil rights struggle of the next century.

"There is less of a problem here than meets the eye."

America's Health Care System Is Not in Crisis

Irwin M. Stelzer

Many commentators, including U.S. president Bill Clinton, cite escalating medical costs and increasing numbers of uninsured people to support their arguments that America's health care system is in crisis and needs to be significantly reformed. In the following viewpoint, Irwin M. Stelzer disputes this view. He contends that neither health care costs nor the number of uninsured citizens are unreasonably high. Stelzer is director of regulatory policy studies at the American Enterprise Institute, a conservative think tank in Washington, D.C., and a columnist for the London *Sunday Times* and the *Boston Herald*.

As you read, consider the following questions:

1. The idea that there is a health care crisis stems from what four sources, according to Stelzer?
2. How does Japan keep its health care costs down, according to the author?
3. According to Stelzer, what percentage of the American population cannot obtain affordable health insurance?

The debate over President Clinton's proposals for reforming our health-care system has been dominated by "experts" and policy wonks who, like the President himself, are never so happy as when they are poring over statistics and the details of this or that new arrangement. The net effect has been to confine discussion to the comparative merits of the Clinton plan as against the single-payer option espoused by certain Democrats, or the four or five other rival reforms espoused by other Democrats or Republicans.

Lost in all this has been the large question of whether a massive transformation of our health-care system is in truth either necessary or desirable. . . .

I wish to ask whether there is something that can legitimately be called a crisis in the provision of health care in America, a crisis so severe as to dictate a thoroughgoing transformation of our system and one which will inevitably involve, at the very least, a huge expansion of government control over a significant sector of our lives and of the American economy.

Four Sources of the Crisis Idea

The idea that there is such a crisis stems, it would appear, from four sources. The first is the insecurity generated by the most recent recession. Most Americans' health insurance is linked to their jobs, with employers paying about 86 percent of the total cost: lose your job, lose your coverage; get a new job and you might not get coverage if you have a health problem. During a period of rising unemployment, enough Americans found this prospect sufficiently unsettling to create a constituency for changes in the way health-insurance coverage is maintained.

Then there is the concern over costs. Already claiming 14 percent of our gross national product—a figure high by international standards—health-care costs have also been rising. Many people have convinced themselves that unless something is done, health care will consume an ever-larger share of GNP, leading in the end to the impoverishment of America.

Additional pressure for reform comes from the notion that *everyone*—no exceptions—should have health insurance as a matter of right. Since somewhere between 37 and 39 million Americans are now widely said to be without coverage, the system must be failing and it must be revamped to provide insurance for all.

A fourth contributor to the sense of crisis is the well-documented liberal bias of the major media. This factor helps to explain one of the great anomalies in the health-care debate: although 75 percent of Americans have been persuaded that there is a crisis (32 percent say the system "needs fundamental changes," and 47 percent that it "needs to be completely rebuilt"), 80 percent simultaneously report *themselves* as "very" or "somewhat" satisfied with the quality and cost of their own health care. "This contradiction," writes Fred Barnes in the premiere issue of *Forbes MediaCritic*, "can be attributed to the media-generated myths that have shaped America's view of its health-care system.". . .

International Comparisons

The approximately $940 billion Americans spent on health care in 1993 did indeed represent a bit more than 14 percent of the nation's total output of goods and services. By what standard is that too much? Three are generally offered: other nations spend less; in the past we ourselves spent less; and the results we get do not justify the amount of money we put in.

But international comparisons—to begin with them—are notoriously flawed. First of all, we are the richest nation in the world, with more houses, cars, telephones, toilets, parks, and other amenities than most other nations can even imagine. As such, we cannot be expected to deploy increments of our rising incomes in the same way as do, say, the Japanese, 54 percent of whom in the average-income bracket still lack indoor toilet facilities (whereas only 1.8 percent of America's *poor* are without such facilities). If we prefer to devote a larger portion of our incomes to top-quality health care, what is wrong with that?

After all, we do not settle for the housing standards that prevail in poorer countries: we insist on central heating and air-conditioning, the latter now installed in nearly half of the homes of even those we classify as poor. Nor are tiny cars with mechanical clutches, common elsewhere, the stuff of which the American dream is made. Neither is spartan health care. Hence we afford ourselves the luxury of making much greater use than other countries do of expensive diagnostic techniques like CAT scans and ultrasound tests.

Another reason why international comparisons mean little is that they give no weight to differences in the quality of service. The *Congressional Quarterly* cites the fact that "Japan's government plays a much greater role in private health-care delivery than does the U.S. government" to explain how "Japan keeps its costs considerably lower than those of the United States." No mention of what Fred Barnes calls "Japanese . . . assembly-line treatment from doctors who see an average of 49 patients a day," and who perform gynecological examinations on scores of women assembled in a single nonprivate room, as physicians scramble to maintain incomes in the face of too-low per-capita reimbursements.

Such stringent government controls on physicians' fees do succeed in lowering the recorded cost of Japanese medical care. But because payment is based on patient visits, the doctor keeps the average length of each visit to five minutes, and the Japanese on average make twelve visits per year, or about three times as many as Americans, whose average visit length is fifteen to twenty minutes. These decreases in convenience for patients, and increases in patient time and travel costs, points out Patricia Danzon of the Wharton School, "are excluded from the national health accounts and from public visibility."

International cost comparisons also ignore queuing and other forms of rationing that reduce recorded costs by forcibly limiting the availability of the service. Like consumer goods in the old Soviet Union, medical services in many of the countries with which America's reformers invidiously compare the U.S. are cheap but hard to get. . . .

Societal Attitudes

Yet another reason why international comparisons are misleading is that they omit societal attitudes. A prominent British physician described to me how decisions are reached in that country about whether to expend resources in an effort to save a seriously damaged newborn, or to let nature take its course. A hospital staff conference, a quiet meeting with the parents, a decision. In America, in similar circumstances, draconian efforts would be made to prolong the child's life. So, too, at other stages of life, including extreme old age.

Indeed, it is the very success of these efforts that contributes to the high cost of health care: the dead are no burden to the system; survivors are. The high expenditures incurred thereby do not result from the greed of doctors (real earnings of American doctors have remained constant for the past fifteen years), or the inefficiency of hospitals, or the swollen profits of insurers, or the price-gouging of drug companies. Rather, they reflect a basic American value—mistaken in the view of certain health-policy experts but deeply held: damn the costs, save lives, and use expensive technologies whenever necessary. . . .

The second basis of comparison offered to support the contention that we are spending too much on health care is our own past. In 1960 we devoted 5 percent of GNP to health care; by 1993 we were up to the famous 14 percent. Yet we do not compare the price of a modern automobile—with automatic transmission, heating, air-conditioning, and stereo tape and CD decks, plus safety features including seat belts, air bags, ABS brakes, and crash-resistant design—with the price of a model-T Ford, and then complain about how much more the new car sells for. So why ignore quality changes in medical care? Indeed, ignoring such quality changes leads to a particularly serious misrepresentation of true costs where medical treatment is concerned. . . .

145

So much, then, for the contentions that international comparisons and cost trends demonstrate that we spend too much on health care. What of the argument that our expenditures seem excessive when stacked up against results?

It is, of course, difficult to gauge just what "bang" we get for our health-care "buck." But the most commonly used standards are infant mortality and life expectancy, and by those America does badly: we seem to buy less life with more money than do other countries. For example, both Canada (10 percent) and Britain (6 percent) spend far less on health care than we do, but life expectancy at birth is higher, and infant mortality lower, in those countries.

Leave aside important questions about the comparability of these figures, and concentrate instead on the implicit assumption that these differences are attributable solely to differences in the efficiencies of the various health-care systems. To accept that hypothesis is to ignore all other influences—in the case of life expectancy, the fact that motor-vehicle deaths per 1,000 population are 28 percent higher in the United States than in Canada, and the fact that Americans consume 20 percent more cholesterol-laden beef and veal than do our neighbors to the north. Not to mention the effect on our longevity figures of the frighteningly high rate of homicide among young blacks.

The Best System in the World

There is no health-care crisis. It's a myth. If millions of seriously ill Americans were being denied medical care, that *would* be a crisis. But that's not happening. Everyone gets health care in this country—the poor, the uninsured, everyone. No, our health-care system isn't perfect. There isn't enough primary care—regular doctor's visits—for many Americans. Emergency rooms are often swamped. The way hospitals and doctors are financed is sometimes bizarre. Health care may (or may not) be too costly. But it's the best health care system in the world—not arguably the best, but the best.

Fred Barnes, *American Spectator*, May 1993.

As for infant mortality, Nicholas Eberstadt of the American Enterprise Institute shows conclusively that the low ranking of the U.S. is attributable to our higher illegitimacy rates (since unwed mothers of all races and in all income groups are more likely to give birth to low-weight babies). Add the disinclination of black women to avail themselves of prenatal care even when it is easily available and free, and the result is an infant-mortality rate that cannot be blamed on the structure of the health-care system.

In short, against the risks inherent in a radical transformation of that system, we cannot expect as probable benefits longer lives and increased infant-survival rates. Those goals *are* achievable, but only by major changes in the way Americans live—i.e., by driving, smoking, eating, and shooting less, and marrying more—and in a welfare system that, unlike our health-care system, has a proven record of failure.

Before leaving this discussion of costs, we should keep in mind an important admonition, offered by Robert Reischauer, director of the Congressional Budget Office:

> The conviction that health-care costs are too high, are rising too rapidly, and are creating undesirable repercussions is a major impetus driving health-care reform. But we also care about access and the continuity of insurance coverage; about the quality and quantity of care we receive; about consumer choice; about our ready access to state-of-the-art treatments, and the pace at which medical technology advances; even about the amenities that have little or no impact on health outcomes.

Which is to say that "costs are not everything." A society as affluent as ours properly insists that noneconomic considerations, including steady progress in the use of expensive technologies that reduce suffering, be given weight.

Insurance Coverage

If there is no crisis in health-care costs, is there one in insurance coverage? Here we come to the second major statistic driving the health-care debate: at some point in 1991, . . . 37 million people were without medical insurance. . . .

Note: these citizens are *not* denied health care, nor do they expire on the steps of hospitals because they cannot produce proof of insurance coverage. For hospital emergency rooms provide care to all comers. In fact, nonprofit hospitals, which constitute 88 percent of those in the U.S., cannot legally turn away any patient needing medical care, or unreasonably deny access to all the modern technology hospitals have available. And not just for the duration of the emergency: the hospital that sets a broken arm for an uninsured patient is obliged to see the treatment through. The care may not be luxurious, but neither is it casual. Per-capita health-care spending on the uninsured, pre-Medicare population is about 60 percent of per-capita expenditures on the insured population—a level sumptuous by the standards of other industrial countries.

Nonetheless, if the 37 million figure did mean what it is often taken to mean—that 15 percent (some estimates are as high as 17.4 percent) of our population lives with the unnerving and continual threat of being unable to pay for medical care—there would certainly be grounds for revising the way we provide medical services.

Fortunately, there is less of a problem here than meets the eye. Some of the uninsured are between jobs; some are students entering the labor market. Katherine Swartz, a specialist in health-care statistics at the Harvard University School of Public Health, points out that most of the uninsured are uninsured for only a short period of time. "Almost half of all uninsured spells end within six months and only about 15 percent of all uninsured spells last more than two years," she told *Congressional Quarterly*. The chronically uninsured group in our society, then, numbers closer to 5.5 million than 37 million people.

And probably fewer than 5.5 million. For not all Americans without insurance find that condition imposed upon them. Only 1 percent of those under the age of sixty-five are uninsurable, according to the Employee Benefit Research Institute. More than half of the uninsured are members of families headed by full-time workers; 40 percent of the uninsured have incomes in excess of $20,000, and 10 percent have incomes in excess of $50,000; only 29 percent are below the poverty level. And those with incomes below $20,000 spend several times as much on entertainment, alcohol, and tobacco as they do on health care, which, says Nicholas Eberstadt, they seem "to treat . . . as an optional but dispensable luxury good." Furthermore, 37 percent of the uninsured are under the age of twenty-five, a generally healthy group—the University of Michigan's Catherine McLaughlin calls them "the young invincibles"—for whom health insurance is often not a cost-effective buy.

If we put all this together—the 15 percent of the uninsured without coverage for two years, plus some who are uninsured for a shorter time, minus those who choose to be uninsured—we come up with a figure of perhaps 3 percent of the population who—although able to obtain health care—cannot obtain affordable health insurance. The policy question thus becomes: should we perform radical surgery on our health-care system for the sake of that 3 percent? . . .

We are left, finally, with a relatively simple set of choices. Everyone agrees that any scheme that would turn 14 percent of the economy over to what the *Economist* calls "a rickety apparatus of new bureaucracies" should be instituted only in response to a major breakdown in the private sector. The proponents of a radical overhaul claim that such a breakdown has occurred. But they are mistaken.

"Our health care mess began . . . when intimacy in the physician-patient relationship became a dispensable item."

Patient-Doctor Intimacy Has Been Sacrificed

Naomi Bluestone

Naomi Bluestone, the author of the following viewpoint, contends that as the health care industry attempts to cut costs and increase its profits, intimacy between health care providers and their patients is being undermined. Bluestone argues that this erosion of physician-patient intimacy—which she believes is a basic human need—will ultimately harm the health care industry by producing demoralized doctors and resentful patients. Bluestone, formerly an assistant commissioner at the New York City Department of Health, runs a private practice of psychiatry in Center Barnstead, New Hampshire.

As you read, consider the following questions:

1. Why is physician-patient intimacy so important, according to the author?
2. What should the country demand of its health care system, according to Bluestone?
3. What unethical and criminal behaviors does the author accuse some doctors of engaging in?

Naomi Bluestone, "The Bottom Line," *JAMA*, vol. 269, no. 19, p. 2580, May 19, 1993.

Everyone's trying to fix it now, but I don't agree with the traditional wisdom of why it broke. My opinion is that our health care mess began not with the advent of space-age technology but when intimacy in the physician-patient relationship became a dispensable item.

The desire for a relatively timeless and private communion that enables the free-flow outpouring of personal suffering is so universal across time and continents, one would think it would not be discarded lightly. But because it is labor intensive and therefore not cost-effective, it has become as disposable as the diaper. The emphasis on efficiency, productivity, and unmonitored cost-accounting now raging out of control in reform circles is sinking us to new depths of patient abuse. The concept of a reasonable cost/benefit ratio, once an overdue adjunct to the provision of good medical care, has deteriorated into a frenzied attempt to convert unlimited spending into a profitable bottom line. This alone seems to be driving the pressure for health care reform. As a result, the baby is being thrown out with the bathwater.

Why has the gold standard of physicians and patients sharing intimate moments in joint inquiry become so quickly relegated to the quaint and nostalgic past of Norman Rockwell? How did our genetically hard-wired need for intimacy, privacy, and trust get so miserably underrepresented in the platforms of those struggling to develop a suitable health care program for this country?

Patient Needs

Surely those who send intimacy to the block have never known the terror of urinating into a toilet bowl that is reddening with arterial blood or the horror of running soapy fingers over a comfortable old breast that has grown a silent, menacing lump. Confidentiality is also being tossed away with the dirty bathwater of the new medicine, a needless luxury to those who do not know the shame disease can cause, or the desire it can arouse to protect one's family from pain. The aggressive but self-deluded young entrepreneurs, who see a growth industry ripe for revolution and therefore up for grabs, could not possibly pursue their rapacious takeover of a wounded profession if they had any sense of how needy and regressed a sick human being generally is and how desperately patients need to share their inner turmoil in a timely way with caring physicians and nurses.

No competitive market of "managers," no universal payer, no innovative distribution technology can succeed if it overrides this basic truth: *Human beings need to relate.* Simply put, sick people will give up their symptoms (a large number of which are somatic displacements) more easily within the protective arms of a trusting relationship. Therefore, we should stop fooling ourselves that a new system built solely on the principles of cost-effectiveness is going to cure our national malaise. We can penalize tertiary surgical subspecialists in favor of primary care until they scream for mama or turn de facto rationing into codified limit setting 'til the cows come home, but what good will it do if time-squeezed family docs lose their inner glow and despise themselves as covert agents of the bottom line?

Honesty, Communication, and Empathy

Brad and Jennifer Webster spare no time and effort when it comes to their children's health.

Because their baby son has health problems, the Costa Mesa, California, couple drive more than an hour to Riverside and two hours to San Diego to take their child to doctors with whom they feel confident—and comfortable.

"I like a doctor who says, 'How are you? How is your son?'" says Jennifer. "They should be concerned for the whole person and the whole family. I'm not saying any doctor is perfect. But our doctors put some effort into the relationship. They have excellent bedside manners. I feel a sense of honesty and integrity. Plus, I feel they are competent."

What the Websters desire from health care—honesty, communication and empathy—are qualities that Americans have generally cherished in relationships with doctors.

Shari Roan, *Los Angeles Times*, September 21, 1993.

Many academicians, economists, legislators, and other federal movers and shakers are currently involved in the restructuring process. A word to the wise: Patients, even though they're manipulated like ciphers, are not fools. They know the difference between a true healer and those who have been assigned that role without the hard-won credentials. They know they've been violated by having to tell their stories and reveal their bodies to multiple screening personnel. They resent opening their wounds over the telephone in the middle of the night to health aides or social workers retrained as bureaucrats, so that they can be routed to some lower-cost practitioner like direct-mail packages with bar codes on their fannies. They are dehumanized and frustrated when they see management trying to reduce human lives to the "short-term" and "long-term" goals of treatment plans that are now issued like manuals of motor-engine repair. They suffer from being trapped defenseless and inarticulate in a system that doesn't hear a word they say. (The great irony, of course, is that if they were less intimidated, they could give the good histories that lessen the necessity for the expensive work-ups that are bankrupting the present system.)

It is troubling that the emerging trends in health care proposals don't reflect the ineradicable need of patients to relate nor do they build in safeguards to protect their right to do so. Sick people and their loved ones will nurse their anger and hatred toward *any* health care plan that offers inadequate surrogates and stumbling blocks. One day their oppression will boil over, and like the peasants of some banana republic they will seize what is theirs by a power higher than Healthcorps or Medipoop.

Demand More

This country should demand more from its planners than equitable and fair redistribution of resources. It should demand more than prenatal care, well-baby clinics, universal coverage, access by rural communities, the demolition of urban slums, and sensible acceptance of impending death. It should not be satisfied until a true healer-patient dyad is made possible no matter what the diagnosis, disability, sickness, or injury. This country, one of the last in the civilized world to address the issue of health care as a social responsibility, needs to learn what every primitive society knows . . . that the shaman and his partner must be protected inviolate, totally free of the laws of economics, sheltered absolutely from intrusion of the world surrounding.

This country also has to demand that we clean up our doctor act before every vestige of trust is lost, because corrupt practitioners will contaminate any new system no matter how tight the controls. There is shameful hanky-panky going on by some morally quirky practitioners in the frantic struggle to beat the encircling noose. Since lack of warm flow on the job breeds pursuit of other rewards, a once reasonably pure profession has been rendered vulnerable.

We all know what's happening. Overt criminality by rogue physicians. Inappropriate submission to coercive and all-pervasive economic pressures by others. "Joint ventures" by the guys in scrub suits who should have stood in their operating rooms. In-kind reactions to escalating claim denials from insurers. Failures in maintaining distance from the pharmaceutical industry. Disciplinary agencies aiming for the wrist instead of the butt. Bad picks by the medical schools. New-age revision of ethical standards. It is these instances of professional failure that give license to the nonclinically oriented reformers who'd throw the baby out *because* of its bathwater.

The clean-up over and credibility restored, we can then address cost containment less ruthlessly and in perspective. We can hearten the decent and honorable physicians, who are daily and in large numbers being driven out of the practice of their profession. They haven't appreciated being treated like sleaze-balls and counterrevolutionaries after a professional lifetime up-holding principles today's managers treat like chicken wings. Demoralized by the debasement of their transcendent, if cur-rently unpopular, values, they do not encourage their kids to subject themselves to the humiliation they have endured: they suggest other ways of making a living and are trying some themselves.

This secession should be a warning to any future health care system coming off the beltway. Healers who have to make sense out of the most horrific details of others' lives deserve to be nur-tured, not taken for granted and abused. Their work (a dirty job, I am tempted to say, but somebody has to do it) is stressful, dif-ficult, and exhausting. If reformers are smart, they will provide a working environment that does not mock their beliefs but rather shows respect for the professional parameters they have established. Only when a dedicated core of respected health professionals is reestablished and permitted to call 'em as they see 'em will reform of the health care system have any substan-tive meaning.

Because when good people opt out, what good is universal ac-cess? Access to what?

"In a serious illness, do we really want Mr. Rogers?"

Patient-Doctor Intimacy Is Not Crucial

Evelyn Storr Smart

In the debate over health care reform, many people place importance on retaining the right to choose their own doctor, fearing that to give up this right would hamper the formation and maintenance of intimate doctor-patient relationships. In the following viewpoint, Evelyn Storr Smart argues that this concern is misplaced. She relates her experience with cancer in order to illustrate her belief that a competent doctor is more valuable than a friendly one. This viewpoint was originally published in the *Los Angeles Times* in July 1993, at which time Smart was a resident of Carmel Valley, California.

As you read, consider the following questions:

1. What does Smart say her cancer was originally diagnosed as?
2. How does Smart say she "chose" her oncologist?

Evelyn Storr Smart, "You Bet Your Life on the Doctor Lottery," *Los Angeles Times*, July 26, 1993. Reprinted by permission of the author.

M_y doctor.

To a lot of people, those words have a metaphysical sound. We want our doctors to be skilled and compassionate, but beyond that we secretly hope that they are also superhuman. The thought of coldly assigning a patient to a doctor like a car to a mechanic is simply appalling.

But is it really?

Many years ago, I lived with my family in a small Midwestern town I later renamed Hysterectomy Village. "Our doctor" was chosen because he was a member of my father's service club. He performed hysterectomies on almost every woman over 35, including my two older sisters, and he got absolutely everyone's tonsils before the age of 5. He was so revered that when he died, a monument was erected in his name in front of the public library.

After moving to California in 1981, I found a doctor through a bridge-playing friend. "He has a terrific personality and is never rushed," she said. Before my first examination, he spent half an hour with me talking about politics and golf. What a great guy, I thought. I'd follow him anywhere. Except Fresno, California, where he moved to be near his grandchildren.

The following month, suffering from a severe case of bursitis, I consulted his replacement, a skinny little kid with a beard. "I believe we'll find calcium deposits in your shoulder, which will probably require surgery."

"No thanks," I said. I left and did the only thing I knew how to do—asked for recommendations from my other bridge-playing buddies.

My Friend's Doctors

Helen's doctor pulled what appeared to be a 2-inch needle out of a drawer. "This is cortisone and Novocaine. I'll inject it directly into the joint and the inflammation will subside." Sarah's doctor prescribed muscle relaxants and instructed me to keep the arm moving to prevent "freezing." Mary's doctor put my arm in a sling and told me not to use it or "the erosion could cause deformity."

All of my friends' doctors had very nice personalities, but the divergence of their opinions was startling. How could I choose? What did I know anyway? I finally picked Doctor No. 3 because he looked like Warren Beatty. And, yes, my shoulder got better. But Dr. Beatty joined a rock group and also moved away.

Now comes the incident that would change the way I feel about doctors for the rest of my life. The doctor I'd been happy with for 10 years (a golfing buddy of my husband's) found a "calcification" in my right breast. For four years, he insisted that it was perfectly harmless. "I'm very aggressive about these

155

things," he said, "but if you were my own wife I'd tell you the same thing. Forget it."

He sat beside me and held my hand for a long time after the pathology report proved him wrong. "Don't worry," he said. "We're in this together." I was grateful for his kind words but couldn't help but think that had I been "assigned" to a better diagnostician, I probably wouldn't be in this at all.

A Big Concern

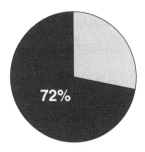

Seventy-two percent of people surveyed in October 1993 were concerned that they might not have good choices of doctors or hospitals under Bill Clinton's health care reform plan.

Source: Survey by ABC News/*Washington Post*, October 7–10, 1993.

One of the greatest objections to a national health-care program is the fear that we won't be able to choose our own doctors. We long for the good old days when doctors made house calls and took the time to get to know their patients. In fact, there is such a demand for these private one-on-one relationships that some medical schools are actively searching for students who majored in the humanities. Family-care doctors are in great demand; patting, touching and maybe even hugging could become a basic part of our medical care.

It would be ludicrous to send every sick person to a specialist. Such indulgence would kill any plan, no matter how many Rhodes scholars worked on it. GP's [general practitioners] can fix most of our problems. But in a serious illness, do we really want Mr. Rogers?

A Matter of Luck

I guess you could say I chose my oncologist. I drew his name from a basket filled with five other names sent to me by the American Cancer Society. By that time, I was convinced that it was all a matter of luck anyway. What does any lay person know about choosing a doctor?

One thing is certain. Had I met him first, I would never have chosen him. He has a lousy personality. He's a super-scientist who works in a university medical center and rarely looks me in the eye; a technocrat who specializes in trying to keep women like me alive for five years or more. You'd think that he was born in that white smock and those nerdy glasses. I don't know if he likes me. He says hello and asks me how I'm feeling. Then he examines me and leaves to consult with other cold fishes who have never seen me.

Sure, it would be nice if he'd sit down and ask about my golf handicap or what books I'm reading. There are times, too, when I could really use a pat on the back or even a hug. But nothing he could say or do could ever make me feel as warm and fuzzy as these four words: "You're still in remission."

I got lucky and drew a good name. And being assigned to a doctor under a national health plan sounds scary. But it was my own choice that got me into the trouble I'm in and may cost me my life.

"The phrase 'managed care.'. . . Look it up in your glossary of contemporary survival and you'll find its true definition: restricted care."

HMOs Do Not Meet Patients' Needs

Vince Passaro

In an effort to control costs, many in the health care industry have embraced the concept of managed care. Under managed care, insurance companies attempt to avoid paying for excessive or unnecessary procedures by regulating the services doctors give to patients. Health maintenance organizations (HMOs) are one type of managed care system. In the following viewpoint, Vince Passaro describes his visit to an HMO to illustrate his view that such organizations provide poor care. Passaro is a fiction writer and the director of communications at Adelphi University in Garden City, New York.

As you read, consider the following questions:

1. According to Passaro, why are insurance companies turning to the managed care concept?
2. How does Passaro describe his HMO doctor?
3. What industries other than health care have been adversely affected by free-market competition, according to the author?

I am not the most wizened veteran of the institutional side of middle-class American life, but even I know enough to run for cover whenever I come across the words "in order to serve you better." The phrase apparently derives from America's conviction that all change is improvement, and it represents an impulse that has systematically removed civility, dignity, and grace from much of our public life. These are the words that herald news of higher life-insurance premiums or function as the opening gambit of letters from your bank informing you that your fees are rising, your interest is shrinking, and your loan accounts are being handed off to a subsidiary from hell ("It is important that we speak with you. If you have a Touch-Tone phone . . .").

Having brought to rubble the ethos of service in such dominions of aggravation as the postal service, the schools, the banks, the supermarkets, and, perhaps, the company you work for, those who would "serve you better" have, as we all know, turned their attention to health care. As with all the other sectors of daily middle-class life made nearly unbearable by bureaucratic obstruction, health care has come before the eyes of the improvers for a very familiar reason: the quest for hard cash. The insurance companies' effort to make more money at your expense relies on the concept of "managed health care," which has become the mantra of the health-care pundits and the ostensible salvation of a system that, despite being irrefutably the best in the world, is considered, largely because of its expense, to be in "crisis." The phrase "managed care" is as thin a verbal fig leaf as "to serve you better." Look it up in your glossary of contemporary survival and you'll find its true definition: restricted care.

The Plunge

In the summer of 1993 my wife and I, with the timing of synchronized swimmers, plunged together into the world of managed care. My wife works for Time Warner, which, as of August 1, switched its employees' coverage to a managed-care program called PruCare, under the direction of Prudential Insurance. In July, it so happened, I had taken a new job as an academic administrator and so, as of August 1, found myself joining one of the cheaper available HMOs, called HIP of Greater New York, which I had signed up for in the mistaken belief that I was required to sign up for some form of medical coverage, even though I was already covered under my wife's plan.

The PruCare plan would be our primary coverage, HIP our backup. At first, PruCare looked like a good deal: Our three children's pediatricians were in the program, as was our family doctor and our superb local pharmacy, where the staff knows us, knows our doctors, and is always quick and helpful. Instead of paying for office visits out of pocket, we would pay a large but reasonable copayment, and even inoculations and well-child visits would be covered. At the pharmacy, we would pay $5 per prescription, regardless of the cost of the drug. My wife would now be paying a higher percentage of the overall cost of the policy, but, with a limit on her contributions of 1¼ percent of her salary, her fees were lower than those I was paying for our superfluous HIP coverage, and lower than those that most other companies these days extort from their employees.

Unhappy News

Alas, even as we joined the program, Prudential was in the process of signing new contracts with its doctors and pharmacies. The first unhappy news arrived almost simultaneously with the start date: as of September 1, presumably having cut a better deal with Pathmark and Duane Reade (massive chains that no doubt promised some cut-rate prices in exchange for the captive market), PruCare would be dropping our pharmacy from its list, and many other mom-and-pop pharmacies like it. For us, living in the city, getting to the nearest Pathmark meant a twenty-minute bus ride out of our neighborhood, not an enticing prospect when we considered we might have sick children in tow. But PruCare, being a "managed" plan, was working from a rigid and surreal formula: it considered a pharmacy in an urban area to be "local" if it lay within two miles of one's residence, perhaps a sensible distance in the suburbs but absurd for city dwellers.

Two or three weeks later we discovered that our pediatricians, and possibly our family doctor, would be leaving the program. Their new contracts had arrived from PruCare, and whereas our doctors had once been paid various set fees for services provided, they were now being moved to a system known as "capitation." In this system the doctor receives a dollar figure per month per patient enrolled in the plan, regardless of whether he or she sees that patient or what amount of care that patient requires—on average, $12 to $14 per month.

Capitation is the ultimate cost-control device: no longer does the insurance company have to fear—heaven forbid!—that a patient is receiving too much care; under capitation it doesn't matter what primary-care doctors do or don't do, for whatever their action they won't be paid a dime extra. If they order up some tests or send a patient to a specialist, the insurance company will have to pay more, but to someone else. Under this arrangement the doctor has an incentive to move patients through as quickly as possible, and will tend to refer cases out rather than begin a prolonged diagnostic effort. To discourage outside tests and referrals, the companies force doctors to get permission by

160

calling representatives who confirm or deny that the procedure ordered is in keeping with their companies' guidelines.

Even these rules, however, prove insufficient to the strictures of cost "management"—that is, some less than absolutely essential care might still get through. The contract therefore provides additional "incentives" (glossary definition: punishments) to encourage doctors to minimize referrals and tests, putting quotas on such activities; exceeding them can lead to further reductions of those already paltry monthly fees.

Do these companies want us to know about these rules? Judging from the PruCare contract, I'd think not. The contract insists on strict secrecy: on no condition is the doctor to discuss the terms of the agreement with the patient, who, either singly or with his employer, pays for it.

Our pediatricians flatly refused to participate in the PruCare plan. Our family doctor amended the more egregious terms of the contract and waited to see if he would be allowed to negotiate. If Time Warner had not left an option for employees to go outside of the network (paying a deductible and 30 percent of the tab), we would have been effectively blocked from consulting the doctors who had been serving us, quite well and at moderate cost, for years.

The First and Last Foray

Meanwhile, over the Labor Day weekend, I made a first—and, it turned out, last—foray into my clinic-style HMO. I had a bronchial infection, I believed (I was right), and our family doctor was away, so I thought I'd give HIP a try. I called their emergency number and was told that one of their "doctors" would be calling me back. Several hours later one did. I described my symptoms, and he agreed that I probably had an infection and could do with an antibiotic. He would fax the weekend clinic, he told me, authorizing my visit.

Not long afterward I arrived at the clinic to find an abandoned-looking corridor with a check-in desk, behind which two men sat watching a tiny television. They waved me on. I stopped in the rest room. In one of the stalls a man was shouting, "The truth *will* come out. All the *lies*, all the *slan*der will be seen clearly in their falsehood. The truth will come out . . . *They* know it will. The truth will come . . ." Et cetera. He kept this up for as long as I was in the bathroom. If you live in New York, you know this guy. Down the corridor was the waiting room, with the usual mauve waiting-room furniture and the usual waiting-room plastic plants. The nurse assistant beckoned me with bored hostility.

"Did you call the emergency help line?" she said. "You're gonna say you did, but I know you didn't."

I had called it, I told her. I told her the "doctor" had said he was faxing authorization for my visit to the clinic.

"I don't know what you're talking about," she said. "We don't have a fax."

"Fine," I said. In the meantime, a shabby-looking older gentleman had come to stand in the open doorway and stare. I nodded at him. He just continued staring, straight into my eyes—one of those looks you associate with the insane.

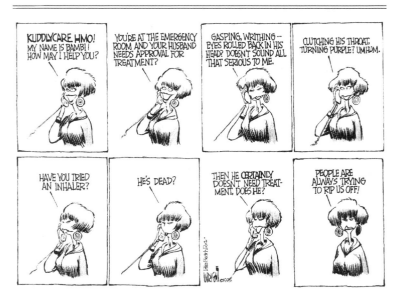

Reprinted by permission: Tribune Media Services.

The assistant asked me if I was taking any medications. She made a snide comment about one of my recent prescriptions. The man in the doorway disappeared, having said nothing. I was sent into a tiny room next door, the examining room, which contained a small desk on which rested only one item, a 1983 pharmaceuticals guide, and an examining table, on which the paper covering, soft and wrinkled, obviously hadn't been changed all day. The windows were frosty with dirt. The staring man entered: he was my doctor. I told him my symptoms; he nodded and approached me with his stethoscope. I began to remove my shirt. "You don't have to," he said. He reached into my shirt, dropped the stethoscope, fished it out again, and listened to one side of my chest. He moved with agonizing slowness. His eyes, I noticed now that we were tête-à-tête, were rather remarkably bloodshot. He wrote a prescription for a weak antibiotic, which was also the cheapest. I told him that this particular antibiotic had never worked when I'd had previous chest infections, and suggested another, far more costly. He just shook his head. I kept thinking of William Burroughs's Dr. Benway, the rummy incompetent and lunatic assassin of *Naked Lunch*. In the end I took his medicine, because it was all I could get, and five weeks later I was almost rid of my cold.

Heaven knows what my employer pays to provide me with this keen service. My contribution, until I dropped the plan, was $119 a month, or $1,400 a year—which I might just as well have spent making a dozen or more visits to good doctors and praying that I didn't have to be hospitalized.

Third World Quality

Those who would improve the public health (all of whom mean "to serve you better") put before us many explanations as to why managed care is the hope of the future, not the least of which is the need for affordable, universally available health care, specifically as proposed by the Clinton Administration. . . . The fundamental issue driving the reform is the need to provide health insurance to the nearly 38 million Americans who don't have it. This is a timely and even noble idea, the only problem being how to pay for it: the best, after all, costs money, and the Clintonites' response, though they could never bring themselves to admit it, has been to devise a third-rate health-care system that everyone can afford.

As a taxpayer and occasionally attentive citizen, I have been hearing that "doctors need to compete like other businesses," that "the market will promote efficiency and quality of care," and so forth, in the belief that the best products and services will, unerringly, rise to the top and the shabbiest will fall by the wayside. Such are the laws of commerce that have given us the American textile industry, American banking, American news-papers, American broadcasting, and American electronics, all in miserable and degraded states. Now, howls the chorus of the free market, let's do it to our medical system.

Yet after my brief introduction to the managed-care system— and the vision it produced of a health-care industry run along the lines of the New York Department of Motor Vehicles—it strikes me that we are bringing the quality of life in America onto a par with that of other unproductive, bureaucracy-strangled, Third World countries, the lands where your money isn't yours and your vote doesn't count.

"The care received by HMO patients is at least as good as that received by other patients."

HMOs Are Beneficial for Patients

Nancy J. Perry

Health maintenance organizations (HMOs) are a type of health care provider company. Many people have criticized HMOs for denying their patients comprehensive—or even adequate—medical treatment in order to control costs. In the following viewpoint, Nancy J. Perry, a senior editor for *Money* magazine, contends that HMOs are economically and medically efficient. While she acknowledges that some patients have had unpleasant experiences dealing with HMOs, she maintains that as a general rule the organizations provide good care at reasonable prices.

As you read, consider the following questions:

1. What percentage of the insured population belonged to HMOs as of the end of 1992, according to Perry?
2. What does the author claim HMOs do to encourage membership?
3. How are doctors paid by HMOs, according to Perry? How does this benefit the patient, in her opinion?

Health maintenance organizations take a startlingly sensible approach to cutting health care costs: Keep people well. Yet the very idea of joining one makes a lot of people sick. Why? HMOs provide health services to members for fixed, prepaid premiums and earn profits only when the costs of treating patients add up to less than those prepaid fees. Therein lies the worry. Many people conjure low-rent, impersonal clinics, interminable delays for appointments, and fatally flawed diagnoses. Yearning for the days of Marcus Welby, they fear HMOs dispense cheap, Doc-in-the-Box medicine that causes more harm than healing.

But it's dawning on millions of Americans that HMOs loom large in their immediate futures. . . . Companies across the country are adopting managed-care plans that reduce costs through contracts with organized provider networks, notably HMOs. Most employees will be forced to use those doctors or pay substantially more out of pocket.

So what's it really like to be in an HMO? Is day-to-day care any good? What do HMO waiting and examining rooms feel like? Do you have easy access to specialists? Should you need open-heart surgery, how trustworthy is the surgeon?

The answer to all of the above: HMOs are better than you think.

At the Forefront

An in-depth investigation by *Fortune* of HMOs around the country, including visits to participating hospitals and medical centers, reviews of clinical outcome studies, and interviews with scores of patients, doctors, and health care experts, yields a surprisingly impressive picture. Most HMO services emphasize primary-care physicians rather than expensive specialists and diagnostic tests. The majority stress prevention and ambulatory care instead of costly hospital stays. Many HMOs not only cut costs but are also medical pioneers. Kaiser Permanente, for instance, has leveraged its huge patient base into a formidable research lab. Such practices put HMOs at the forefront of trends shaping the health care industry.

One of the oldest HMOs, Kaiser was founded a half-century ago by industrialist Henry J. Kaiser. During World War II, he offered a prepaid health plan to his 200,000 workers and their families at Kaiser's plants and shipyards on the West Coast. When the war ended, at the behest of local unions Kaiser began accepting members from the entire community. In California, where Kaiser is headquartered, some 41% of the insured population are HMO members [as of June 1993]. Kaiser remains a model HMO, with 12 affiliated groups around the country employing 9,000 doctors who look after 6.6 million patients.

While less popular in the East than on the West Coast, the

HMO concept is spreading. At the end of 1992, 41 million Americans—19% of the insured population—belonged to one of America's 550 HMOs, up from six million in 1976. Several studies, including a survey of 90,000 consumers by the private National Research Corp., show that satisfaction with HMOs is actually higher than patient approval in other health insurance programs. Says Lee Kamenow, 73, a member of FHP in Beverly Hills, who was diagnosed with a brain tumor just after joining: "The doctor there saved my life."

"An Incredible Bargain"

Managed care, of course, is a catchall term for a range of health care plans. The key difference among them is how much freedom of choice patients have. Point-of-service (POS) plans, for instance, are a fast-growing type of HMO that permit members to receive treatment from both participating and nonparticipating doctors. But they must pay extra if they go outside the network. Classic HMOs are the most restrictive of the lot, tightly controlling costs by limiting access to doctors, specialists, and hospitals.

Quality and Cost

Membership today in managed-care health plans has topped 50 million. . . . Why?

Quality. It must come first. Without quality care, there is no way HMO membership would have grown so dramatically. Eighty-five percent of all HMO physicians are board certified, compared to 61% of practicing physicians nationwide in 1993.

Cost. HMO costs are frequently 20% below standard insurers. We've been successful in wringing out tremendous inefficiencies and waste.

Westcott W. Price III, *Los Angeles Times*, March 14, 1995.

To encourage membership, HMOs generally require no deductible and no insurance claim forms and charge members only a small "co-payment"—usually $3 to $10—for drugs and office visits. Kaiser's plain-vanilla package, with $5 co-payments, includes doctor visits, hospitalization, lab tests, and other basics for about $430 a month for a family in the Mid-Atlantic region with any number of children (rates vary by location). Preventive care such as mammograms, children's immunizations, and cholesterol screenings are free. On average, employers pick up 88% of the premium for an individual employee and about 75%

of family coverage. The balance is paid by the employee.

By contrast, employees with fee-for-service insurance are seeing their annual deductibles rise to as much as $1,000 and are required to pay more of the medical bills than before. Concludes Helen Darling, manager of health care programs at Xerox, where 63% of employees are now in HMOs: "An employee contributes $6.33 per month after the company-paid premium for individual coverage and gets comprehensive benefits, typically with prescription drugs. That's an incredible bargain."

Doctors will need to get with the HMO program too. Those who refuse will likely find themselves losing patients and watching afternoon reruns of *St. Elsewhere*. Today, 79% of all HMOs employ practitioners who see HMO as well as private patients in the doctors' own offices. Says Dr. Anthony Hedley, a renowned orthopedic surgeon at the Institute for Bone and Joint Disorders in Phoenix: "HMOs should never cease recruiting better doctors, because they'll join. Personally, I want to remain active and have always participated."

Of course, HMO horror stories do exist. One irate Manhattan member, Jeffrey Richter, 30, a musician, says that shortly after joining U.S. Healthcare he got a severe flu and was running a temperature. He called 13 doctors on the approved "provider" list, couldn't get one to see him, and ended up driving with a 103-degree fever to the suburbs to see his mother's doctor. Explains a busy physician who treats only private patients: "I'm in at 7:30 A.M. and I stay here until ten at night. You think I'd do that on a salary? You've gotta be kidding. If my income was capped, I'd come in at nine and leave at five."

Then there's the tale of the wealthy businessman with a knee problem. After waiting three hours past the appointed time to finally see an orthopedic surgeon, the businessman learned the doctor had lost all his files. He walked out. The punch line: This doctor worked for the prestigious Mayo Clinic. Notes Dr. Jesse Jampol, medical director of Health Insurance Plan (HIP) of Greater New York, a large HMO: "If you're in Blue Cross/Blue Shield and have a problem with a doctor, you blame the doctor. If you're in HIP, you blame the system."

Setting the Record Straight

To set the record straight, most HMO waiting rooms are not filled with characters who wandered off the set of *Les Miserables*. HMOs run the same gamut as do private-doctor offices with patients who look like you and me. HIP, for example, operates plush Manhattan medical centers filled with commercial-banker types as well as nondescript Long Island clinics where equipment crowds the narrow corridors.

Kaiser has the feel of good, old-fashioned, slightly chaotic medicine, where salaried doctors care more about outcomes than incomes. Says Dr. John Miles, area director of the Southern California Permanente Medical Group, who joined Kaiser as a "temporary job" in 1955: "This is an idealistic way to practice medicine, without worrying about running an office or charging patients." Family-practice doctors on HMO staffs do pretty well, typically earning $100,000 or so annually.

Less Costly Alternatives

Today's fee-for-service system encourages the health care industry to inflate costs. Insurers pay doctors and hospitals more money for doing more procedures, whether or not more procedures benefit patients. Since third parties pay the bills, most insured employees have little reason to consider cost when seeking care. . . .

Managed care organizations provide less costly alternatives to the present system. Such organizations—for example, Kaiser Permanente in California and the Harvard Community Health Plan—offer all the care one needs for a fixed price per person per month. They hire or contract with doctors and hospitals, and organize and monitor treatment. Their premiums reflect their ability to control costs while providing high-quality care.

Alain C. Enthoven and Richard Kronick, *New York Times*, June 12, 1994.

Checking into FHP's hospital in Fountain Valley, California, on the other hand, feels like being initiated into a corporate headquarters operation. In a sleek, marble-floored lobby, men and women in business suits hurry everywhere, and the place hums with efficient operations. FHP's landscaped, 16-acre "campus" is a gleaming center for one-stop medical shopping: You need a dermatologist? Glasses? Chemotherapy? Drugs? Step right up. A "mixed model" HMO, FHP employs 1,000 staff doctors who work full-time for the HMO and contracts with an additional 7,000 private practitioners in five states and Guam who treat both HMO and private patients. . . .

The Benefit of All

Private doctors who work for HMOs usually receive a fixed monthly "capitation" payment for each HMO patient under their care. Often, if the physician can provide care for less, he keeps part of the difference. This financial arrangement, which rewards doctors for cutting costs, raises all the questions about quality of care. In their zeal to spend less than they earn, charge critics, HMO doctors are bound to scrimp on care by refusing to send patients for expensive diagnostic tests or other special treatment. Says one disgruntled FHP Medicare patient who quit the plan after less than a year: "I'd pick them up for false advertising. They give you a long list of specialists. Then when you try to see them, it's another story."

HMO doctors do wait to see results of their treatment when problems are "nonurgent"—to the benefit of all concerned. Whether you have lower back pain or a headache, they point out, a two-week wait for an X-ray or magnetic resonance imaging (MRI) scan usually won't hurt. It could, however, help by saving you from unnecessary procedures. Says Dr. Thomas Reardan, a trustee of the American Medical Association who has started supplementing his private practice with HMO patients: "You start thinking, 'If I do this test, will it change the way I'm going to treat a patient?' If not, I don't use the test. In the end, it's the morals and ethics of physicians that will make the system work."

Research backs him up. Clinical studies done at UCLA, Harvard, the University of Texas, Brigham and Women's Hospital, and other research centers compared diagnoses, treatment, results, and mortality rates for people with illnesses such as cancer, hypertension, diabetes, and heart disease. Results show that the care received by HMO patients is at least as good as that received by other patients.

The strength of HMOs—as well as their greatest weakness—lies in their numbers: At Kaiser, for instance, there are only 1.4 doctors per 1,000 patients. That compares with a national average of about 2.5 per 1,000 patients. And it explains why it may take three months to get an appointment for an ordinary physical.

But visit Kaiser's neurological center in Redwood City, California, and you find an X-ray lab teeming with patients waiting for mammograms, ultrasounds, and MRI tests. Says Brenda Wiley, who has worked as a Kaiser X-ray technician for almost seven years: "You do 30 mammographies a day and you get pretty good at it. Doctors who don't deal with enough patients get dull. They may never see a brain stem tumor. We see ten a year. And if they don't grasp what it is, because they haven't been exposed to it, that could be fatal."

Doctors with poor performance records are fired. Says Dr. Gary Goldstein, FHP's chief medical executive: "We are regulated by 80 local, state, and federal agencies. In the fee-for-service world, you don't know your doctor's malpractice history or even if he has a degree. Nobody oversees that guy."

To provide companies and consumers with an additional quality check, the National Committee for Quality Assurance, a nonprofit, national accreditation organization for managed-care plans, has approved rigorous accreditation standards for HMOs. So far, 53 companies, including PacifiCare of Southern California, Prudential, and U.S. Healthcare, have received accreditation. Reviews are pending for 127 more [as of June 1993].

Fine, you say, but what happens when something goes seriously wrong? What if I want treatment at the Mayo Clinic or Sloan-Kettering? In most cases, the answer is: You can choose only medical facilities affiliated with the HMO unless you're in a point-of-service plan. Generally, upon joining an HMO, you choose or are assigned a primary-care physician who acts as a "gatekeeper," deciding when you need a specialist and who that specialist should be. If you insist on seeing a specialist outside the system, you'll pay the full price of the visit.

While certainly a drawback, such a system is not as onerous as it sounds. A good general practitioner is capable of handling most patient problems for a lot less than a specialist will charge. To expand the nation's paltry pool of generalists, Kaiser and FHP have started postgraduate residency programs to train more primary-care physicians, not just in hospitals but also in doctors' offices, where most patients receive care. . . .

Ultimately, the best way to remain healthy as an HMO member is to ask the right questions up-front. Should problems arise, says Glenn Meister, an employee benefits consultant with Foster Higgins, "the company human resources department can help." Better yet, pick a physician you trust. In the efficient new world of managed care, your family doctor must be your best advocate.

Periodical Bibliography

The following articles have been selected to supplement the diverse views presented in this chapter. Addresses are provided for periodicals not indexed in the *Readers' Guide to Periodical Literature*, the *Alternative Press Index*, or the *Social Sciences Index*.

Fred Barnes	"What Health-Care Crisis?" *American Spectator*, May 1993.
Michael V. Buenaflor	"What Unhappy Patients Taught Me About HMOs," *American Medical News*, October 25, 1993. Available from 515 N. State St., Chicago, IL 60610.
Sara Collins	"Desperate for Doctors," *U.S. News & World Report*, September 20, 1993.
Edmund Faltermayer	"Getting Health Alliances Right," *Fortune*, May 16, 1994.
Glamour	"Women and Health Care: Don't Let This Moment Pass," February 1994.
William V. Healey	"Barbarians at the Gate," *Wall Street Journal*, September 24, 1993.
Michael A. Hiltzik and David R. Olmos	"A Mixed Diagnosis for HMOs," *Los Angeles Times*, August 27, 1995. Available from Reprints, Times Mirror Square, Los Angeles, CA 90053.
Charles B. Inlander	"The Hovering Vultures: How Greedy Physicians Prey upon Patients," *USA Today*, July 1993.
New York Times	"Second Opinions," special section on health care reform, June 12, 1994.
Robert A. Nordgren	"The Case Against Managed Care and for a Single-Payer System," *JAMA*, January 4, 1995. Available from 515 N. State St., Chicago, IL 60610.
Joyce Price	"Are Hospitals Injurious to Your Health?" *Insight*, July 24, 1995. Available from 3600 New York Ave. NE, Washington, DC 20002.
David Spiegel	"Compassion Is the Best Medicine," *New York Times*, January 10, 1994.
Ellyn E. Spragins	"Beware Your HMO," *Newsweek*, October 23, 1995.
Joseph D. Wassersug	"Don't Deify the Role of Gatekeeper," *American Medical News*, May 24–31, 1993.
Murray Weidenbaum	"A New Look at Health Care Reform," *Vital Speeches of the Day*, April 1, 1995.

For Further Discussion

Chapter 1

1. The Beef Industry Council claims that beef is a necessary part of a healthy diet, while Neal D. Barnard promotes a meat-free diet as the healthiest. The Beef Industry Council is part of the National Live Stock and Meat Board, which promotes beef consumption. Neal D. Barnard is a physician. Does the background of the authors affect the credibility of their viewpoints? Why or why not?

2. Nathaniel Mead claims that the benefits of milk consumption are exaggerated and that milk actually causes many health problems. What evidence does he use to support his argument? Kathleen Meister argues that the absence of milk in the diet, especially that of children, can lead to health problems. What evidence does she use to support her argument? Whose viewpoint do you find more compelling? Why?

3. Geoffrey Cowley maintains that using vitamin supplements can ward off a host of serious illnesses caused by vitamin deficiencies. What arguments does Ruth Kava employ to question the efficacy and safety of vitamin supplements?

4. Each pair of viewpoints in this chapter presents diametrically opposed opinions about the health benefits of a certain item. Are there ways of reconciling these opposed points of view? If so, what might they be? Do the viewpoints themselves suggest any methods?

5. How do the viewpoints in this chapter correspond to your dietary choices? Is any of the evidence presented in this chapter likely to change your dietary habits? If so, why?

Chapter 2

1. Susan Chollar maintains that exercise can alleviate psychological depression. What arguments do Rebecca Prussin and her colleagues present against using exercise as a treatment for depression? Are their arguments persuasive? Why or why not?

2. The viewpoints by both Chollar and Prussin and her colleagues use anecdotal examples to support their arguments. Which viewpoint uses this technique most effectively? Explain your answer. Which viewpoint uses scientific research most effectively? Support your answer with examples.

3. David Stipp contends that obesity is a disease that requires treatment. Sally E. Smith argues that obesity is a natural condition and that defining it as a disease stigmatizes overweight people. Based on your reading of these viewpoints, do you think obesity is a disease? Why or why not?

4. Stipp is a senior writer for *Fortune*, a national business magazine. Smith is the executive director of the National Association to Advance Fat Acceptance, an organization that combats discrimination against overweight people. Does knowing their professional affiliations affect your assessment of their arguments? If so, explain how.

Chapter 3

1. Marlene Cimons uses mostly anecdotal evidence to assert that alternative remedies are viable. Robert L. Park and Ursula Goodenough contend that proponents' reliance on primarily anecdotal evidence indicates that there is a problem with alternative treatments. Whose viewpoint do you find more effective, and why? Why do you think that so many people are drawn to using alternative medicine when there is little scientific evidence to support its use?

2. According to Nancy Bruning, not even the proponents of homeopathy can explain how it works. Nevertheless, she argues, homeopathy is an effective alternative therapy. Does her inability to explain how homeopathy works affect her argument? Why or why not? Do you believe that Stephen Barrett successfully counters Bruning's claims? Explain your answer.

3. Roger Walsh and Nathaniel Mead both address the possible effects of meditation on individual health. Compare and contrast each author's characterization of meditation and health. Whose depiction is more effective? Why?

4. Rosemary Ellen Guiley seriously advocates prayer as a solution to even the most hopeless medical situation. William B. Lindley's tone is questioning and perhaps even scornful. Neither presents statistical, scientific evidence to prove his or her point. Whose rhetorical style do you find more effective? Why? Do you think the lack of scientific evidence affects either author's argument? Explain.

5. After reading the viewpoints in this chapter, are you more or less likely to try alternative treatments for medical problems? Explain your reasoning.

Chapter 4

1. Nancy F. McKenzie's viewpoint originally appeared in the *Nation*, a left-wing political magazine. Irwin M. Stelzer's viewpoint originally appeared in *Commentary*, a conservative magazine. Can you find evidence of the political orientations of these magazines in the viewpoints? Give one example from each viewpoint.

2. Naomi Bluestone argues that intimacy is essential in the patient-doctor relationship. Evelyn Storr Smart contends that a doctor's competency is more important than his or her amiability. Whose argument do you find most compelling? Why?

3. In her viewpoint, Bluestone writes as a member of the medical profession. Smart, on the other hand, writes of her experiences as a patient. Which author do you believe is most qualified to evaluate the importance of patient-doctor intimacy? Why? With which author do you most agree? Explain your answer.

Organizations to Contact

The editors have compiled the following list of organizations concerned with the issues debated in this book. The descriptions are derived from materials provided by the organizations. All have publications or information available for interested readers. The list was compiled on the date of publication of the present volume; names, addresses, and phone numbers may change. Be aware that many organizations take several weeks or longer to respond to inquiries, so allow as much time as possible.

American Chiropractic Association (ACA)
1701 Clarendon Blvd.
Arlington, VA 22209
(800) 986-4636
fax: (703) 243-2593

ACA promotes legislation defining chiropractic health care and works to increase the public's awareness and use of chiropractic medicine. Its publications include the monthly *Journal of Chiropractic* and the monthly newsletter *ACA/Today*.

American College of Sports Medicine (ACSM)
PO Box 1440
Indianapolis, IN 46206-1440
(317) 637-9200
fax: (317) 634-7817

ACSM conducts research on sports medicine and exercise science to discover how they can enhance physical performance, fitness, and health. It publishes the quarterly newsletter *Sports Medicine Bulletin*, the monthly journal *Medicine and Science in Sports and Exercise*, the *ACSM Fitness Book*, and various monographs in its annual *Exercise and Sport Sciences Review*.

American Council on Science and Health (ACSH)
1995 Broadway, 2nd Fl.
New York, NY 10023-5860
(212) 362-7044
fax: (212) 362-4919

ACSH provides consumers with scientifically balanced evaluations of food, chemicals, the environment, and human health. It publishes the quarterly magazine *Priorities: For Long Life and Good Health*, the semiannual *News from ACSH*, the book *Issues in Nutrition*, and the booklets *America's Health: A Century of Progress* and *Vitamins and Minerals: Does the Evidence Justify Supplements?*

American Dietetic Association (ADA)

216 W. Jackson Blvd., Suite 800
Chicago, IL 60606
(312) 899-0040
fax: (312) 899-1979

ADA is the largest organization of food and nutrition professionals in the United States. It works to shape the food choices and nutritional status of the public for optimal nutrition, health, and well-being. The association publishes the monthly *Journal of the American Dietetic Association* as well as a variety of booklets, pamphlets, and fact sheets about nutrition.

American Holistic Medical Association (AHMA)

4101 Lake Boone Trail, Suite 201
Raleigh, NC 27607
(919) 787-5146
fax: (919) 787-4916

AHMA promotes the practice of holistic health care, a concept that emphasizes the integration of physical, mental, emotional, and spiritual concerns with environmental harmony. Its publications include the quarterly journal *Holistic Medicine*, the books *Fitness Guidelines* and *Nutritional Guidelines*, and a variety of brochures.

American Medical Association (AMA)

515 N. State St.
Chicago, IL 60610
(312) 464-4818
fax: (312) 464-4184

The AMA is the primary professional association of physicians in the United States. Founded in 1847, it disseminates information to its members and the public concerning medical breakthroughs, medical and health legislation, educational standards for physicians, and other issues concerning medicine and health care. The AMA operates a library and offers many publications, including the weekly *JAMA: The Journal of the American Medical Association*, the weekly newspaper *American Medical News*, and journals covering specific medical specialties.

American Public Health Association (APHA)

1015 15th St. NW
Washington, DC 20005
(202) 789-5600
fax: (202) 789-5681

APHA works to protect and promote personal, mental, and environmental health by establishing standards and researching public health issues. In addition to books, manuals, and pamphlets, the association's publications service offers the monthly *American Journal of Public Health* and the *Nation's Health*, which is published ten times per year.

American Society of Law, Medicine, and Ethics (ASLME)
765 Commonwealth Ave., Suite 1634
Boston, MA 02215
(617) 262-4990
fax: (617) 437-7596
e-mail: aslme@bu.edu

ASLME members include physicians, attorneys, health care administrators, and others interested in the relationship between law and medicine and in health law. The organization has an information clearinghouse and a library. It publishes the quarterlies *American Journal of Law and Medicine* and the *Journal of Law, Medicine, and Ethics*.

The Heritage Foundation
214 Massachusetts Ave. NE
Washington, DC 20002
(202) 546-4400

The Heritage Foundation is a public policy research institute that supports limited government and the free market system. It opposes nationalized health care and has proposed its own health care reform plan that minimizes government involvement. The foundation publishes the quarterly journal *Policy Review* as well as monographs, books, and papers concerning health care in America.

National Association to Advance Fat Acceptance (NAAFA)
PO Box 188620
Sacramento, CA 95818
(916) 558-6880
fax: (916) 558-6881

NAAFA works through public education and activism to end weight-based discrimination and to improve the quality of life for overweight people. The association provides information about the disadvantages of weight-loss treatments and publishes the bimonthly *NAAFA Newsletter*.

National Cattlemen's Beef Association (NCBA)
444 N. Michigan Ave.
Chicago, IL 60611
(312) 467-5520
fax: (312) 467-9729

NCBA is a service organization for livestock marketers, growers, meat packers, food retailers, and food service firms. It works to promote and educate the public about the meat industry, beef nutrition, and food safety. NCBA publishes the *Food and Nutrition News* five times per year, as well as numerous brochures and pamphlets.

National Strength and Conditioning Association (NSCA)
PO Box 38909
Colorado Springs, CO 80937-8909
(719) 632-6722
fax: (719) 632-6367

NSCA encourages the use of strength and conditioning techniques for improved physical performance. It publishes the bimonthly journal *Strength and Conditioning*, the quarterly *Journal of Strength and Conditioning Research*, and the bimonthly newsletter *NSCA Bulletin*.

North American Vegetarian Society (NAVS)
PO Box 72
Dolgeville, NY 13329
(518) 568-7970
fax: (518) 568-7636

NAVS works to educate the public and the media about the nutritional, economical, ecological, and ethical benefits of a vegetarian diet. Its publications include the quarterly magazine *Vegetarian Voice* and the books *Good Nutrition: A Look at Vegetarian Basics*, *Vegetarianism: Answers to the Most Commonly Asked Questions*, and *Vegetarianism: Tipping the Scales for the Environment*.

Office of Alternative Medicine (OAM)
National Institutes of Health
6120 Executive Blvd., Suite 450
Rockville, MD 20892-9904
(301) 402-2466
fax: (301) 402-4741

The Office of Alternative Medicine is a division of the National Institutes of Health, the principal biomedical research agency for the U.S. government. The OAM evaluates alternative medical treatments to determine their effectiveness and to help integrate effective treatments into mainstream medical practice. It supplies the public with information on diet, meditation, homeopathic and chiropractic medicine, therapeutic touch therapies, and herbal treatments. The office has published the report *Alternative Medicine: Expanding Medical Horizons*, which details the status of alternative therapies in the United States.

U.S. Food and Drug Administration (FDA)
Center for Food Safety and Applied Nutrition
HFS-555, Rm. 5809
200 C St. SW
Washington, DC 20204
(800) FDA-4010

The FDA is a consumer protection agency that is responsible for inspecting foods and drugs to ensure their quality and safety. Through its Center for Food Safety and Applied Nutrition, the FDA researches and develops standards for the quality, nutrition, and safety of foods and drugs. Publications available from the FDA and the Center for Food Safety and Applied Nutrition include the magazine *FDA Consumer* and the information packets *FDA: Safeguarding America's Health*, *Facts About Weight Loss: Products and Programs*, *Nutrition and the Elderly*, and *Vegetarian Diets: The Pluses and the Pitfalls*.

Bibliography of Books

Barbara Faye Abrams — *Women, Nutrition, and Health*. St. Louis: Mosby-Year Book, 1993.

Edward E. Abramson — *Emotional Eating: A Practical Guide to Taking Control*. New York: Lexington Books, 1993.

Jeanne Achterberg — *Woman as Healer*. Boston: Shambhala Publications, 1990.

Lu Ann Aday — *At Risk in America: The Health and Health Care Needs of Vulnerable Populations in the United States*. San Francisco: Jossey-Bass, 1993.

John Ankerberg — *Can You Trust Your Doctor? The Complete Guide to New Age Medicine and Its Threat to Your Family*. Brentwood, TN: Wolgemuth & Hyatt, 1991.

Marc Ian Barasch — *The Healing Path: A Soul Approach to Illness*. New York: Putnam, 1993.

Stephen Barrett — *The Vitamin Pushers: How the "Health Food" Industry Is Selling America a Bill of Goods*. Amherst, NY: Prometheus Books, 1994.

Stephen Barrett and William Jarvis — *The Health Robbers: A Close Look at Quackery in America*. Amherst, NY: Prometheus Books, 1993.

Lisa Belkin — *First, Do No Harm*. New York: Simon & Schuster, 1993.

Francie M. Berg — *The Health Risks of Weight Loss*. Hettinger, ND: Healthy Weight Journal, 1994.

Walt Bogdanich — *The Great White Lie: Dishonesty, Waste, and Incompetence in the Medical Community*. New York: Simon & Schuster, 1991.

Robert Buckman and Karl Sabbagh — *Magic or Medicine? An Investigation of Healing and Healers*. Amherst, NY: Prometheus Books, 1995.

Hugh Burroughs — *Alternative Healing: The Complete A–Z Guide to over 160 Different Alternative Therapies*. La Mesa, CA: Halcyon, 1993.

Burton Goldberg Group — *Alternative Medicine: The Definitive Guide*. Puyallup, WA: Future Medicine, 1993.

Kurt Butler — *A Consumer's Guide to "Alternative Medicine": A Close Look at Homeopathy, Acupuncture, Faith Healing, and Other Unconventional Treatments*. Buffalo: Prometheus Books, 1992.

Sandra Cabot	*The Body-Shaping Diet*. New York: Warner Books, 1995.
California Department of Education	*Vegetarian Diets and Related Content: Giving and Receiving Messages, Dietary Guidelines for Americans, Vegetarian Principles and Practices*. Sacramento: California Department of Education, 1995.
Daniel Callahan	*The Troubled Dream of Life: Living with Mortality*. New York: Touchstone, 1994.
David N. Camaione	*Fitness Management*. Dubuque, IA: Brown & Benchmark, 1993.
Marie Cargill	*Acupuncture: A Viable Medical Alternative*. Westport, CT: Praeger, 1994.
Ellington Darden	*Living Longer Stronger*. New York: Berkley, 1995.
Department of Veterans Affairs	*Nine Steps to a Healthy Weight*. Washington, DC: Dept. of Veterans Affairs, 1992.
Harris Dienstfrey	*Where the Mind Meets the Body*. New York: HarperCollins, 1991.
Rod K. Dishman, ed.	*Advances in Exercise Adherence*. Champaign, IL: Human Kinetics Publishers, 1994.
Doug Dollemore et al.	*New Choices in Natural Healing: Over 1,800 of the Best Self-Help Remedies from the World of Alternative Medicine*. Emmaus, PA: Rodale Press, 1995.
Annette Dula and Sara Goering, eds.	*"It Just Ain't Fair": The Ethics of Health Care for African Americans*. Westport, CT: Praeger, 1994.
James Eden	*Energetic Healing: The Merging of Ancient and Modern Medical Practices*. New York: Insight Books, 1993.
Miguel A. Faria Jr.	*Vandals at the Gates of Medicine: Historic Perspectives on the Battle over Health Care Reform*. Macon, GA: Hacienda Publishing, 1995.
Emily R. Foster	*Fitness Fun*. Champaign, IL: Human Kinetics Publishers, 1992.
Edward L. Fox	*The Physiological Basis for Exercise and Sport*. Madison, WI: Brown & Benchmark, 1993.
Fred M. Frohock	*Healing Powers: Alternative Medicine, Spiritual Communities, and the State*. Chicago: University of Chicago Press, 1992.
Delores A. Gaut and Anne Boykin, eds.	*Caring as Healing: Renewal Through Hope*. New York: National League for Nursing, 1994.
Richard Grossinger	*Homeopathy: An Introduction for Skeptics and Beginners*. Berkeley, CA: North Atlantic Books, 1993.

Harold D. Hafs and Robert G. Zimbelman, eds.	*Low-Fat Meats: Design Strategies and Human Implications*. San Diego: Academic Press, 1994.
George C. Halvorson	*Strong Medicine*. New York: Random House, 1993.
Richard and Rachael Heller	*Healthy for Life*. New York: Dutton, 1995.
David Hilfiker	*Not All of Us Are Saints: A Doctor's Journey with the Poor*. New York: Hill and Wang, 1994.
Jane R. Hirschmann	*When Women Stop Hating Their Bodies: Freeing Yourself from Food and Weight Obsession*. New York: Fawcett Columbine, 1995.
Oscar Janiger	*A Different Kind of Healing: Doctors Speak Candidly About Their Successes with Alternative Medicine*. New York: Putnam, 1993.
Steven Jonas	*Regular Exercise: A Handbook for Clinical Practice*. New York: Springer, 1995.
Jon Kabat-Zinn	*Wherever You Go, There You Are: Mindfulness Meditation in Everyday Life*. New York: Hyperion, 1994.
Nicholas J. Karolides	*Focus on Fitness: A Reference Handbook*. Santa Barbara, CA: ABC-Clio, 1993.
Jeanne Kassler	*Bitter Medicine: Greed and Chaos in American Health Care*. New York: Carol Publishing, 1994.
Frank I. Katch	*Introduction to Nutrition, Exercise, and Health*. Philadelphia: Lea & Febiger, 1993.
Phikkhu Khantipalo	*Calm and Insight: A Buddhist Manual for Meditators*. London: Curzon, 1994.
Paula Kurtzweil	*Making It Easier to Shed Pounds*. Rockville, MD: Dept. of Health and Human Services, Public Health Service, Food and Drug Administration, 1995.
Dave Lindorff	*Marketplace Medicine: The Rise of the For-Profit Hospital Chains*. New York: Bantam, 1992.
Giovanni Maciocia	*The Practice of Chinese Medicine: The Treatment of Diseases with Acupuncture and Chinese Herbs*. New York: Churchill Livingstone, 1994.
Mary Briody Mahowald	*Women and Children in Health Care: An Unequal Majority*. New York: Oxford University Press, 1993.
James Marti	*The Alternative Health and Medicine Encyclopedia*. New York: Gale Research, 1995.

Nancy F. McKenzie, ed.	*Beyond Crisis: Confronting Health Care in the United States*. New York: Meridian, 1994.
Bill Moyers	*Healing and the Mind*. New York: Doubleday, 1993.
National Institutes of Health, National Cancer Institute	*Your Best Body: A Story About Losing Weight*. Bethesda, MD: 1994.
National Institutes of Health, National Heart, Lung, and Blood Institute	*Exercise and Your Heart: A Guide to Physical Activity*. Bethesda, MD: 1993.
Bonnie Blair O'Connor	*Healing Traditions: Alternative Medicine and the Health Professions*. Philadelphia: University of Pennsylvania Press, 1995.
P. Berry Ottaway, ed.	*The Technology of Vitamins in Food*. New York: Blackie Academic & Professional, 1993.
Russell R. Pate and Richard C. Hohn, eds.	*Health and Fitness Through Physical Education*. Champaign, IL: Human Kinetics Publishers, 1994.
Lynn Payer	*Disease Mongers: How Doctors, Drug Companies, and Insurers Are Making You Feel Sick*. New York: Wiley, 1992.
Jamie Pope	*The Last Five Pounds: How to Lose Them and Leave Them Forever*. New York: Pocket Books, 1995.
Susan Powter	*Food!* New York: Simon & Schuster, 1995.
Susan Powter	*Stop the Insanity!* New York: Simon & Schuster, 1993.
Jack Raso	*Alternative Health Care: A Comprehensive Guide*. Amherst, NY: Prometheus Books, 1994.
Elyse Resch and Evelyn Tribole	*Intuitive Eating: A Recovery Book for the Chronic Dieter*. New York: St. Martin's Press, 1995.
Carolyn Reuben	*Antioxidants: Your Complete Guide: Fight Cancer and Heart Disease, Improve Your Memory, and Slow the Aging Process*. Rocklin, CA: Prima, 1995.
Neil Rolde	*Your Money or Your Health: America's Cruel, Bureaucratic, and Horrendously Expensive Health Care System: How It Got That Way and What to Do About It!* New York: Paragon House, 1992.
John R. Romans et al.	*The Meat We Eat*. Danville, IL: Interstate Publishers, 1994.
Roy J. Shephard	*Aerobic Fitness and Health*. Champaign, IL: Human Kinetics Publishers, 1994.

Frederick J. Simoons | *Eat Not This Flesh: Food Avoidances from Prehistory to the Present*. Madison: University of Wisconsin Press, 1994.

Petr Skrabanek and James McCormick | *Follies and Fallacies in Medicine*. Buffalo: Prometheus Books, 1990.

Colin Spencer | *The Heretic's Feast: A History of Vegetarianism*. London: Fourth Estate, 1993.

Martin A. Strosberg et al., eds. | *Rationing America's Medical Care: The Oregon Plan and Beyond.* Washington, DC: Brookings Institution, 1992.

Thich Nhat-Hanh | *The Blooming of a Lotus: Guided Meditation Exercises for Healing and Transformation*. Boston: Beacon Press, 1993.

James E. Tillotson | *America's Foods, Health Messages and Claims: Scientific, Regulatory, and Legal Issues*. Boca Raton, FL: CRC Press, 1993.

Abraham Verghese | *My Own Country: A Doctor's Story of a Town and Its People in the Age of AIDS*. New York: Simon & Schuster, 1994.

Debra Waterhouse | *Outsmarting the Female Fat Cell*. New York: Hyperion, 1993.

Andrew Weil | *Spontaneous Healing.* New York: Knopf, 1995.

Elizabeth M. Whelan and Fredrick J. Stare | *Panic in the Pantry: Facts and Fallacies About the Food You Buy*. Buffalo: Prometheus Books, 1992.

Timothy P. White | *The Wellness Guide to Lifelong Fitness*. New York: Rebus, 1993.

Index

ABC News/Washington Post poll, 156
ACT UP (AIDS Coalition to Unleash Power), 141
acupuncture, 93, 94, 95
African Americans, 33, 57, 138, 139, 146-47
AIDS, 76, 139, 141
Akil, Huda, 66
alcohol, 20, 24
allergies, 26, 29
  less common than supposed, 32, 36
alternative therapies
  are less expensive than traditional medicine, 94, 98
  are valid, 92-96
    con, 97-100
  combined with conventional treatments, 93-94, 106
  have long histories, 95
American Academy of Pediatrics, 30, 34, 36
American Cancer Society, 156
American College of Sports Medicine (ACSM), 55, 59
American Council on Science and Health (ACSH), 44, 46, 50
American Enterprise Institute, 146
American Home Products (AHP), 80, 81
American Journal of Cardiology, 22
American Medical Association (AMA), 93, 102, 169
American Spectator, 146
Amgen, 75
amphetamines, 76-77, 80
anemia, 30, 32, 39
anencephaly, 39
antibiotics, 28, 99
Aronne, Dr., 76, 78
arthritis, 23, 26, 29, 30
asthma, 26, 29, 118

Baar, Karen, 94
Barnard, Neal D., 21
Barnes, Fred, 144, 146
Barrett, Stephen, 99, 107
Beasley, Joseph, 28
Beef Industry Council, 17
Benor, Daniel J., 127, 131
benzocaine, 86
Biochemical Corporation, 76
Biological Homeopathic Industries

(BHI), 111
Biological Therapy: Journal of Natural Medicine, 111, 112
Blackburn, George, 84
Block, Gladys, 42
Bluestone, Naomi, 149
bovine serum albumin (BSA), 30
bovine somatotropin (BST), 28
Blumberg, Jeffrey, 39
Brooklyn College, 63
Bruning, Nancy, 101, 104
Bunai, Russell, 26, 29, 30

caffeine, 24
Cain, Sarah, 63, 66
Canada, 146
cancer, 23, 43, 48, 56, 155-57
  and alternative medicine, 99
  and folic acid, 39, 41
  and milk/vitamin D consumption, 26-28, 30, 41
  vitamins may prevent, 42
Case, Andrea Golaine, 33
Center for the Study of Human Nutrition and Aging (Tufts University), 39
Centers for Disease Control and Prevention (CDC), 55, 88
childhood immunization, 140
Chinese herbs, 95
cholesterol, 19, 20, 42, 47, 85
  is present only in animal products, 24, 32
Chollar, Susan, 62
Christians, 129, 131
Christian Science, 129, 131
Cimons, Marlene, 92
Clarkson-Smith, Louise, 64
Clinton, Bill, 138, 143
Cohen, Jerome, 38
Collins, Sara, 139
Committee for the Scientific Investigation of Claims of the Paranormal (CSICOP), 132
Community Health Care Association, 139
Congressional Quarterly, 144, 148
Consumer Reports, 110
coronary heart disease, 32, 43, 76
  and meditation, 116
  and physical activity, 56, 57, 60
Cowley, Geoffrey, 37

184

tuberculosis (TB), 28, 140

Ullman, Dana, 103, 112
United States, 29, 78, 93, 102
  Congress, 98, 108, 113
  Congressional Budget Office, 147
  Department of Agriculture (USDA)
    Agriculture Handbook, 20
    Dietary Guidelines, 18, 22, 23-24
  Department of Health and Human
    Services, 18
  health services in, 139, 141
  and increased life expectancy, 49-50
  infant mortality rate in, 146-47
  and motor vehicle deaths, 146
  Public Health Service, 39
  sedentary population of, 56, 57
  wealth of, 144
University of Alabama, 39
University of California, 41, 43, 80,
  114, 116, 169
University of Michigan, 148
University of Western Australia, 63
University of Wisconsin, 139
USA Weekend, 116
U.S. Healthcare, 167, 170
U.S. News & World Report, 77, 139

vitamins and minerals
  as antioxidants, 41-42, 48
    may be neutral or harmful for
      some, 50
  are chemicals, 39, 45, 47-48
  beta carotene, 38, 40, 47, 48
    and cancer, 42
    and cardiovascular disease, 43
    increased sales of, 41
  calcium, 24, 35, 46
    helps prevent osteoporosis, 40, 50
    present in green vegetables, 27
  folic acid (B vitamin), 39, 41
  iron, 18, 30, 32, 46, 47
  niacin, 18, 46

safe/toxic levels of, 46
sources/benefits of, 40
vitamin A, 41, 45
vitamin B, 18, 38, 41, 46
vitamin C, 41, 42, 48, 49
  may reduce heart attack risk, 43
  side effects of overdose, 46, 47
vitamin D, 34-35
  could prevent breast cancer, 38
  and rickets, 28, 39, 41
vitamin E, 38, 41, 42, 48
  can help prevent heart disease, 38
vitamin supplements
  benefits of, 37-43
  are unproven, 44-50
  dangers of, 45-47

Wadden, Thomas, 84
Wall Street Journal, 130
Walsh, Roger, 114
weight loss
  commercial industry for, 78, 83, 86
    exploits low self-esteem, 84, 87
  treatments
    are beneficial, 74-71
      because obesity is a disease,
        75-76
      because obesity is genetic, 78
    are harmful, 82-88
      and ineffective, 76, 85, 86, 87
      and should be better regulated
        by government, 86-88
    dexfenfluramine, 80, 81
    fenphen, 76, 79, 85
    side effects of, 79-80, 81
Weinstein, Corey, 102
Willett, Walter, 38
Winn, James R., 80
World Health Organization, 93
Worrall, Ambrose, 127

Ziegler, Regina, 42